STAMI[barcode]ON EVERY CHILD'S HEART

IMPULSIVE BEHAVIOR

"... I WILL SAVE YOUR CHILDREN." — ISAIAH 49:25

REBECCA DAWSON

BLUE ROOM PUBLICATIONS AND PRODUCTION, LLC

STAMPED ON EVERY CHILD'S HEART: IMPULSIVE BEHAVIOR

 BLUE ROOM PUBLICATIONS AND PRODUCTION, LLC
www.blueroompublications.com
P.O. Box 1837 Warsaw, IN 46581

Copyright ©2013 by Rebecca Dawson
ISBN 978-0-615-82982-1

Library of Congress 2013942042
Dawson, Rebecca.
Stamped on Every Child's Heart: Impulsive Behavior / Rebecca Dawson – 1st ed.
ISBN 978-0-615-82982-1
1. Christian Living. 2. Parenting. 3. Counseling and Recovery.

Unless otherwise noted, Scripture references are taken from The Holy Bible, English Standard Version® (ESV®) Copyright © 2001 by Crossway, a publishing ministry of Good News Publishers. All rights reserved. Used by permission.

Scripture references marked CEV are from the Contemporary English Version®, Copyright © 1995, American Bible Society. All rights reserved.

Scripture references marked MSG are from THE MESSAGE, copyright © 1993. 1994, 1995, 1996, 2001, 2002. Used by permission of NavPress Publishing Group.

Scripture references marked NIRV are from the Holy Bible, NEW INTERNATIONAL READER'S VERSION®. Copyright © 1996, 1998 Biblica. All rights reserved throughout the world. Used by permission of Biblica.

Scripture references marked NIV are from THE HOLY BIBLE, NEW INTERNATIONAL VERSION®. NIV®. Copyright © 1973, 1978, 1984 by International Bible Society. Used by permission of Zondervan. All rights reserved.

Scripture references marked NLT are from the Holy Bible New Living Translation, Copyright © 1996. Used by permission of Tyndale House Publishers, Wheaton, Illinois, 60189. All rights reserved.

Scripture references marked TLB are from The Living Bible, Copyright © 1971 by Tyndale House Publishers, Wheaton Illinois, 60187. All rights reserved.

Scripture quotations taken from the Amplified® Bible, Copyright © 1954, 1958, 1962, 1964, 1965, 1987 by The Lockman Foundation. All rights reserved. Used by permission. (www.Lockman.org)

Design and Layout: Joshua Petrillo

Printed in the United States of America

Dedicated to my husband,
Chad.
Thank you!

CONTENTS

NOTE FROM THE AUTHOR

The hope of this material is to equip you in handling tough issues facing your child. It is not necessary to be a trained therapist to apply these truths. However, my hope is that these truths will in fact transition into therapy and impact those who provide care. These truths are created for praying parents, grandparents, counselors, friends, teachers, or anyone who wants to stamp biblical understanding and practical application upon the hearts of children everywhere. The Word of God offers healing. My prayer is that it will bring healing to you and your child.

My hope is to assist you in handling obstacles and to encourage a better relationship between you and your child. You are the one with the relationship with *this child*, so you know him or her best. My purpose in providing this information is to expand your biblical knowledge, while enhancing your relationships and healing brokenness. Remember, relationships take time to develop. This is your time to teach your child, and I want to help you with that.

Prayerfully yours,
Rebecca

INTRODUCTION

Christians often use secular psychological techniques when grappling through issues. We employ the same methods as the world while expecting different results. However, we live entirely different from the world (or we should). Yet, we expect the same strategies to apply to our pain. We use the world's approaches and try popular suggestions. These things are not necessarily wrong. Solid secular methods do exist, but they rarely apply biblical knowledge. As Christ-followers, we have an entirely separate resource to tap into, the Word of God. This Word of Truth offers to be the Bread of Life if we are willing to live by it.

Is there more for the Christian community? Do we utilize the extra tools we have access to? Do we truly believe that God's Word is alive and active and able to help us in our deepest need? Do we live that way? The Scripture references its ability to pull down strongholds. The Word of God is powerful and living. "For the word of God is... sharper than any two-edged sword, piercing to the division of soul and of spirit, of joints and of marrow, and discerning the thoughts and intentions of the heart" (Hebrews 4:12, ESV). "For no word from God will ever fail" (Luke 1:37, NIV). If we truly believe the Word of God is capable of doing all this, then why don't we live our lives that way? This material strives to combine secular methods with biblical principles in hopes of stamping greater love and understanding upon you and the heart of your child.

A series emerged as I developed this book. What started as training for young counselors became a tool for parents. Then what began as one book transitioned into many. Within these books, I hope to encourage parents and those who work with young people who are grappling with tough behaviors and issues. Each book is meant to equip parents to never walk alone or feel their hands are tied in any given situation. Because I love Impulsive Peter, we will start there. Nonetheless, each book has a special message to share. May each book fall into your hands at exactly the right moment, and may they help illuminate your path.

CHAPTER 1
YOUR CHILD, YOUR OFFERING
Offering your child as a sacrifice

Lord, Today, I am involved in the life of a child. A child You know by name. I dedicate this child to You. He (she) is my offering. This child needs Your healing and care. Help me to make a difference in his (her) life. May it all be to Your glory. In Jesus' name, Amen.

"Be prepared. You're up against far more than you can handle on your own" (Ephesians 6:13, MSG). Yes, you are up against more than you can handle as a parent, as a counselor, as a grandparent, as a teacher, or as a friend! Loving a child well takes work, a lot of work. Parents may feel overwhelmed by the demands of this world as they attempt to guide their children through this maze we call life. Now, couple that with daily frustrations and some kind of disorder, and you have a full plate. Despite all that, remember, you are not alone. Many people face mountains too difficult to scale on their own strength, but thankfully, God is able to help (Ephesians 3:20).

When your plate is full and exhaustion overwhelms you, where do you begin? "Above all, keep loving one another earnestly, since love covers a multitude of sins" (1 Peter 4:8). Start with stamping love on your child's heart. God's love can transform hearts and circumstances. Let's look at ways to increase your love for your child through truth. It may not lead us where we expected, but ultimately God's ways are not our own (Isaiah 55:8).

Stamping is the creative art of making something beautiful out of ordinary materials. It takes a creative approach, utilizing what exists. The artist may begin bewildered, overwhelmed, and not sure where to start in this creative process. Believing God's promises sometimes starts the same way. For some, God's promises seem too good to be true. That's where faith steps in, "Faith is confidence in what we hope for and assurance about what we do not see" (Hebrews 11:1, NIV). God uses faith to create the extraordinary from the ordinary. Stamping provides us with imagery from which we can learn. What may feel overwhelming can transform into something creatively, wonderful, and unexpected. Faith will help you get there.

Abraham and Sarah, an infertile elderly couple, had one of the greatest faith walks in history (Genesis 17:15-26). They waited years for God to grant His promise of a child. Our God keeps His promises even when circumstances appear doubtful. Hebrews 10:23 says, "For he who promised is faithful." "The LORD was gracious to Sarah, just as he had said he would be. He did for Sarah what he had promised to do" (Genesis 21:1, NIRV). Sarah was over 90 years old, and Abraham had waited more than 100 years when God finally delivered His promise of a child. Have you ever thought God was acting too slowly? Or have you grown tired waiting for His promises to be fulfilled? Have you ever waited 100 years for God's response? Abraham did, and God responded. It takes a lot of strength to exercise faith. Abraham was granted strength in his feeble, 100-year-old body, as he flexed his faith muscles. Isaac's birth probably seemed like the

THE GREATEST OF LOVE STORIES START WITH SACRIFICE.

completion of Abraham's bucket list. Now they were set, but that's not the end of the story. Ultimately, God would ask the unimaginable of Abraham. "Then God said, 'Take your son, your only son. He is the one you love. Take Isaac. Go to Moriah. Give him to me there as a burnt offering. Sacrifice him on one of the mountains...'" (Genesis 22:2, NIRV). The greatest of love stories start with sacrifice (John 3:16; John 15:13; 1 John 3:16).

What were the steps for Abraham to fully accept God's will and then obey with radical love (Genesis 22:3)? We know very little about Abraham's thoughts at this point. Can you imagine? This would have been a gut-wrenching, heart-aching, anguish that pulled on every fiber of his parental being. If you have ever spent time pleading with God on behalf of your child, you might understand. Decisions are not easy when life hangs in the balance, especially if those decisions involve the life of a child. Do moms that choose to release their child to adoption feel as Abraham must have? Adoption is truly a gift of sacrifice and love, especially for the parent who surrenders her child in hopes of a better future, a hopeful, better life that will no longer include her. Sacrificial acts of love are not easily implemented or forgotten.

Now, can you imagine how deeply Abraham's faith was tested? There is a big difference between accepting God's command and obeying it. And there's also a huge gap between believing and receiving the gift God promised and then being asked to give it back. The Scriptures say, "By faith Abraham, when he was tested, offered up Isaac, and he who had received the promises was in the act of offering up his only son... He considered that God was able even to raise him from the dead, from which, figuratively speaking, he did receive him back" (Hebrews 11:17, 19). Our promises are delivered the same way: in God's timing and with His plan. The Bible says, "In your heart you plan your life. But the LORD decides where your steps will take you" (Proverbs 16:9, NIRV). What is the purpose of promises? They are meant to bless us. However, the blessing should not stop there. We receive the promises for our benefit and then to bless others like Abraham (Genesis 12:2). The Apostle Paul encourages believers with these words: "Then you can always give freely. We will take your many gifts to the people who need them. And they will give thanks to God" (2 Corinthians 9:11, NIRV).

Why are we blessed to bless others? Because obedient acts direct others toward God. Our blessings point others to Jesus just as caring does. "The Father is a merciful God, who always gives us comfort. He comforts us when we are in trouble, so that we can share that same comfort with others in trouble" (2 Corinthians 1:3-4, CEV).

God alone possesses the ability to heal and tenderly comfort (Psalm 103:3; 2 Corinthians 1:7; Psalm 103:3). Comforting another can also be used to encourage similar blessings. What has God called you to do for *this child*? Is it really God speaking? Do you know for sure? The Bible says, "… His sheep follow him because they know his voice. But they will never follow a stranger. In fact, they will run away from him. They don't recognize a stranger's voice" (John 10:4-5, NIRV). If you are being asked to sacrificially act on behalf of *this child*, you know your calling. It may be hard. But, however difficult it may be, continue. *Your child is worth it.*

TRUSTING GOD WILL PROVIDE

Abraham's son, Isaac, helped to build the altar his dad would soon place him on. As they worked, young Isaac spoke to his dad. Abraham replied, "'Here I am, my son'" (Genesis 22:7). Abraham was there for this child. He was present. This is a great example to us whether you are a parent, grandparent, counselor, teacher, or friend. Be there for the children in your life. Be available, be ready, and *be there*! Abraham, in the midst of facing his greatest trial, remained present with his son. He wasn't wrapped up in his career, escaping to Twitter, or allowing anything else to dictate his life. Are you called to anything less with your child? God will instruct you and counsel you as you are involved in the life of *this child* (Psalm 32:8, NIV). He promises He will never leave you alone on this journey (Deuteronomy 31:8).

BE THERE FOR THE CHILDREN IN YOUR LIFE.

Trusting God can be like climbing aboard a stagecoach in the old Wild West. You inspect the team of horses set to take you on a journey. Your eyes move to the empty seat up top beside the driver. Quickly assessing the look in his eyes, you know that seat is not available. At least, not for you. Reluctantly, you climb aboard the coach. It's dark and dank inside as you fumble for a seat. The musty aroma almost sends you packing and has you second-guessing this entire thing. Suddenly, you feel the horses jerking. It's time to go. You take a seat more out of necessity than desire, and the journey gets underway. Then, you realize that your back faces the coach's wall. Your back faces your future. Your destination lies in the hands of the driver and his team of horses. You don't know the way. Besides, you're sitting in the dark. You can't see anyway. Will you get there? Will there be attacks? You have heard stories of vicious assaults. Maybe you should turn around? Instead, you realize that you must blindly trust this man and his team to lead you or you may never arrive.

Similarly, it is with blind faith that the Christian walk proceeds. The reassurance that God alone is God enables us to trust. "Trust in the Lord with all your heart, and do not lean on your own understanding. In all your ways acknowledge him, and he will make straight your paths" (Proverbs 3:5-6). Our lives are not in the hands of a blind driver. Our lives are in the hands of Almighty God and *so is the life of your child.*

Abraham's trust-story continues when Isaac questions, "Where is the lamb?" Abraham replies, "'God will provide for himself the lamb for a burnt offering, my son.' So they went both of them together" (Genesis 22:8). God will provide. A lamb was needed for the sacrifice, and Isaac was the intended lamb.

Where does your trust-story begin? We must trust. God will come through. He will provide... something. Without trust, our paths cannot be straight. If you want to lead your child on straight paths, you must start with trusting God. Many people lack trust in God, and I am no exception. If you lack trust, ask God to give you faith. It truly is that simple (Matthew 7:7; Mark 9:24).

Abraham does not reveal details or the expected outcome to his child. When I plan events for our boys, I rarely tell them until the time arrives. Just in case something changes because our plans are usually meant for fun. Abraham, a trusting father, withheld the details of the sacrifice. There was nothing fun about this moment for Abraham. Who would want to tell their child this? Yet a thread of hope remains within Abraham as he speaks to Isaac. Abraham is hoping God will provide for him as He had in the past. Abraham continues trusting.

God did not need Abraham, but He called Abraham to this act of obedience. He also calls us to obedience for our own good. As humbling as it may be to realize it, God truly does not need us. Nonetheless, God loves us and chooses to use us. We need to be obedient as Abraham was. When we obey God, we are most useful to Him, and we get to play a part in His plan. Being used by God is an *awesome* experience! Is God calling you to trust Him with an obedient act on behalf of *this child*?

When was the last time you felt that God used you—or have you ever been used by God? As a parent, a counselor, or a friend, you can regularly be used by God in the life of *this child*. However, you must remain obedient. God does not need you, but He wants you to be a part of His plan. If you lack obedience, you may miss the role God wants you to play. It all starts with your first move, a trust move. Will you trust? This can be incredible both for you and your child.

IT ALL STARTS WITH YOUR FIRST MOVE, A TRUST MOVE.

ALTERED MOMENTS

What words could Abraham offer to Isaac, and how could he even keep his composure? Isaac was as good as dead as he lay upon the altar. This experience could have caused him to be a really messed-up kid. By today's standard, Isaac would have likely been a good candidate for Post Traumatic Stress Disorder. Abraham had built the altar, laid Isaac upon it, bound him to it, and was about to kill his son.

Some of you may also feel as if you were placed on an altar and left for dead by those you trusted. Or perhaps *this child* has been placed on an altar somewhere by someone that he trusted. Kids who have been placed upon altars may appear to be as good as dead. By all appearances, it is all over for them. *This child*, or you in some cases, appears to be a goner. But then, God steps in! God is not shaken by appearances. He does not judge circumstances as we do. God has Isaac's back even when the circumstances look daunting and without hope. God can *always* provide. What Satan intends for evil, God can use for good (Genesis 45:4-9; 50:20).

Isaac's precise age at the time of this event is uncertain. Regardless of his exact age, however, we can be sure he was old enough to understand what his dad was doing. I cannot imagine tying up my two-year-old. How could he not be filled with fear and confusion as I bound him? Or what about my nine-year-old who has a greater understanding? I'm sure I couldn't have convinced him that my actions were done in love. As for my seven-year-old, he would have run, and I don't think I could have stopped him. What was Isaac thinking? What was he doing? Was he protesting, screaming, weeping, or fighting back? Did he sit by quietly as his father tied ropes around his body? Would you? Was he pleading, "Dad, what are you doing? Dad? Please don't do this! Daaaad!"

Have you ever held a knife over someone? Think for a moment. Our actions carry great weight. What about a figurative knife and using it hatefully? Your intent may never have been to murder anyone, but was it being used to hurt someone's feeling, to seek revenge, or to steal something that did not belong to you? The Bible says, "Anyone who hates a brother or sister is a murderer, and you know that no murderer has eternal life residing in him" (1 John 3:15, NIV). So again, I ask, "Have you ever held a 'figurative' knife against anyone?"

> *The trouble is with me, for I am all too human, a slave to sin. I don't really understand myself, for I want to do what is right, but I don't do it. Instead, I do what I hate... And I know that nothing good lives in me, that is, in my sinful nature. I want to do what is right, but I can't* (Romans 7:14-18, NLT).

If you have placed anyone on an altar or been there yourself, then you understand. Sin is great. We need help. The hope for our future is the Lord. What has been placed upon the altar in the past needs to stay upon the altar. Leave the past behind, learn from it, and move forward (Hebrews 6:1, NIV). Freedom starts there.

JUST SHOW UP

Remember, this was a test, only a test (Genesis 22:1). Sometimes it is all about the test. Ever forget to study for a test? I once dreamed that I was back in school and failed to study for a test. Those around me seemed to pass with ease, but I failed miserably. So I asked to retake the test the next day. I didn't want to fail (even if it was only a dream). Sometimes by failing we meet the same challenges until we are prepared to retake the test.

It's no wonder that the Israelites wandered aimlessly for 40 years. They had failed God's tests and kept going around the same mountains. If you feel like you have been wandering around the same obstacles for years, it may be time to retake the test. But prepare this time.

We have been conditioned from childhood to know the importance of taking a test. But what do you do when the test is from God? Abraham could have given 150 reasons why he could not follow through with this test. Or he could have waited for the right circumstances and the right time (Ecclesiastes 11:4, NLT). He could have done 150 other things, but he didn't. Instead, he obeyed, and that opened up an opportunity for God to do His thing. Abraham was prepared to complete this gut-wrenching act of obedience. He was prepared for the test. Abraham was willing to obey even at the cost of his child. But, God did not require that. God acknowledged his obedience. Blessings came from Abraham's obedience. The act of obedience by itself is a blessing to God. Is God asking something difficult of you? Something that seems impossible, maybe even outrageous? Maybe He is asking the unbelievable of you only to say, "Ok, you did what I asked. Now watch me show up!" Exodus 14:14 eloquently offers this perspective, "The LORD will fight for you, and you have only to be silent." I love that imagery. Yet how many of us stand by quietly allowing the Almighty to fight for us? Sometimes we merely need to show up and wait.

"To obey is better than sacrifice" according to 1 Samuel 15:22. Are you withholding anything from God? Your fears? Your pride? Your failures or inadequacies? Your success or accolades? Your dreams? *This child*? Are you keeping anything from God? Withhold nothing from Him. To give everything to God means placing all things on the altar, including the life of *this child*. Metaphorically, placing your child on the altar takes the focus off of you and your ability to help. It offers the proper perspective, and places the focus on what God is able to do. God is rightfully the only one capable of doing life-changing work in *this child*. He has a restoration plan in mind. Restoration becomes possible when you give your child back to Him. Remember, He gave *this child* to you in the first place. Now your responsibility is to place *this child* back with Him. Place your child willingly before the Maker saying, "I come in obedience to You, Lord. You love *this child* more than I do. Please help me. Help *this child* to live!"

Giving your child back to God gives Him the opportunity to provide for both of you. This may occur in moments marked by pain, but God can still provide. The Hebrew word translated "provide" may also mean "see" or "see to it." God *sees* your child and will provide.

SPIRITUALLY DEAD

1 Kings 17:17-22

In America, the land of the free and the home of the brave, children should lack for nothing. Unfortunately, that is not the case. According to the Children's Defense fund (2013),[1] *every day* in America:

4	children are killed by abuse or neglect.
5	children or teens commit suicide.
24	children or teens die from accidents.
208	children are arrested for violent crimes.
467	children are arrested for drug crimes.
914	babies are born to teen mothers.
2,712	babies are born into poverty.
4,500	children are arrested.

What is happening to our children? Could some of these tragedies be the result of a spiritual deadness within our society? Certainly those who perpetrate crimes upon children are spiritually dead (Galatians 5:19-21). Which raises the question, what does it mean to be spiritually dead?
A child that is spiritually dead obviously lacks the Spirit of God. Children possess a sinful nature just like adults, resulting in spiritual deadness. Children are also under attack

whether it is by depression, low self-esteem, anger, shame, abuse, or neglect. Such attacks can stand in the way of a child's learning about Jesus and prevent them from coming into spiritual life. These difficulties can get in a child's way and weigh him or her down. Consequently, the spiritually dead generally have no one leading them to the truth. So they usually continue to live life as though *dead*. Don't let that be said of you or *this child*.

The Bible refers to life in the land of the living (Psalm 27:13; Psalm 142:5). Life is intended to be lived. But for whatever reason, many never experience life that way. Those that are spiritually dead may appear to be sleeping through life. This may be like someone living life, but just going through the motions. Ephesians 5:14 says, "Awake, O sleeper, and arise from the dead, and Christ will shine on you." Ephesians 5:14-17 in *The Message* translates this way:

Don't waste your time on useless work, mere busywork, the barren pursuits of darkness. Expose these things for the shame they are. It's a scandal when people waste their lives on things they must do in the darkness where no one will see. Rip the cover off those frauds and see how attractive they look in the light of Christ. Wake up from your sleep, climb out of your coffins; Christ will show you the light! So watch your step. Use your head. Make the most of every chance you get. These are desperate times! Don't live carelessly, unthinkingly. Make sure you understand what the Master wants.

In the story of 1 Kings 17, God illustrated for us the spiritually dead. In this story a widowed mother, her son, and the prophet Elijah lived life based on faith. This mom provided food for Elijah in a famine when she had nothing. She did not have a lot to offer. But she did have faith, and God never let her supply lack. Later, this mom would grieve over the death of her child, which she believed to be a result of her own sin. She said to Elijah, "What have you against me, O man of God? You have come to me to bring my sin to remembrance and to cause the death of my son!" (1 Kings 17:18). Like any loving parent, the widow first blamed herself. Many parents do the same, questioning, "What did I do? Is my past still haunting me?" The grieving widow felt as if the sins of her past had mounted up against her, and this time had taken her most precious possession, her child.

IF YOU ARE WONDERING IF YOUR CHILD'S SPIRITUAL DEADNESS IS A RESULT OF YOUR SIN, THEN FOCUS UPON THE CHARACTER OF GOD.

Was her child's death a result of her sin? For greater understanding, reflect upon Elijah's prayer.

> *O God, my God, why have you brought this terrible thing on this widow who has opened her home to me? Why have you killed her son?' Three times he stretched himself out full-length on the boy, praying with all his might, 'God, my God, put breath back into this boy's body!' God listened to Elijah's prayer and put breath back into his body—he was alive!* (1 Kings 17:19-23, MSG).

If you are wondering if your child's spiritual deadness is a result of your sin, then focus upon the character of God. "He does not treat us as our sins deserve or repay us according to our iniquities" (Psalm 103:10, NIV). God is forgiving if we ask (1 John 1:9). God is also willing to carry your concerns because He cares about you and *this child* (1 Peter 5:7). He is a God willing to tenderly comfort (2 Corinthians 1:7, TLB). Our hope continues because God is able to transform lives. "We shall not all sleep, but we shall all be changed" (1 Corinthians 15:51). He can restore the spiritually dead and give life. God causes those sleeping to rise—*whether it's you or your child.*

IT'S A JOB TO HELP A CHILD

How does God restore the lives of children? He does it by using people like you. He uses people that participate, that challenge, that shape what He has created. He uses individuals that care. He uses people like you, people who are willing to act on behalf of *this child.* God uses individuals that will intercede.

God did restore the life of the young man in 1 Kings 17. However, someone had to be willing to intercede on the child's behalf. Someone needed to be willing to fulfill their role in God's restoration plan for the boy. Someone had to get into the trenches called life and fight for *this child.* You have been given a similar opportunity. As it was said of Israel in the Old Testament, so it might be said of you today, "The Lord set his love on you and chose you" (Deuteronomy 7:7). You are chosen. Whether you are a parent, counselor, teacher, or friend, God has placed you in the life of *this child* for a reason.

You have a role to fulfill. But ultimately, you decide whether you will make a difference in this child's life. We all have a choice. What will your choice be?

In the story of Elijah, he laid himself upon the child three times and cried out to the Lord. Why three times? The number of times may not be as important as his willingness to persist. In the restoration battle, healing will probably take more than one attempt. One try may not be sufficient. Do not give up after a single attempt. Elijah kept going. You, likewise, will need to keep going (Galatians 6:9).

IN THE RESTORATION BATTLE, HEALING WILL PROBABLY TAKE MORE THAN ONE ATTEMPT.

In the end, God listened to Elijah, and life was restored to the child (1 Kings 17:22). All children need someone praying for them to be restored, but not every child has someone. If you are a teacher, counselor, grandparent, or friend, you are not being asked to parent *this child*. Rather, you have the opportunity to impact the life of *this child* through influence, involvement, and prayer. You have the ability to display Jesus, the one who can restore life and replenish souls. This calling is an honor. At times, *this child* may view you as a parent because you might offer things he or she has never experienced before (e.g., time, attention, affirmation, prayers, and love). Yes, it is a big responsibility for a parent or a friend. But do not be afraid of it. If everyone responded with fear, then very few people would be helped. Jesus said,

> *And anyone who welcomes a little child like this on my behalf is welcoming me. But if you cause one of these little ones who trusts in me to fall into sin, it would be better for you to have a large millstone tied around your neck and be drowned in the depths of the sea* (Matthew 18:5-6, NLT).

Proceed in humility and in love, but proceed.

THE HEART OF THE MATTER

In 1970, Maslow, an American psychologist, created a hierarchy of needs. He believed certain needs must be met in order to reach full developmental potential. Physiological needs, including food, shelter, water, and warmth were listed first. His triangular needs continued with safety, love and belonging, self-esteem, and self-actualization. According to Maslow in order to feel love, physiological needs must first be met.[2] Is that true? What do we truly desire? "Every man longs for love that never fails" (Proverbs 19:22, NIRV). Scripture also tells us that, "[God] has planted eternity in the human heart" (Ecclesiastes 3:11, NLT). We all desire God's steadfast love within our hearts, including *this child*. Stamp love upon a child's heart and life will begin to be restored.

CHAPTER 2
PREPARATION
Ephesians 6:10-19 and Joshua 6:1-16, 20

What does it mean to prepare for battle? It can be like a war these days to be a parent. If you have not noticed lately, then take a good look around. The media, entertainment, and in some cases your child's classroom, bombard your child's worldview every day with a worldly ideology. These views challenge your son or daughter to adopt a similar approach to the world. Whether you believe it or not, your child is creating his or her worldview largely from the world they live in and are exposed to. Take one look at the world today, and tell me that should not be a major concern on every parent's heart. So is it a battle? First Timothy 6:20 says, "Guard the deposit entrusted to you." Your child is deposited into your care for a short season, but also for a reason. You are instructed to guard *this child*. It starts with you. Are you up for this?

Being a parent is a tiring job. Truly, parenting is not for the faint of heart. That is why I believe God chose you. You are exactly what this child needs. Do not *give up*! There are already too many tired parents. But keep in mind, your child is worth it. Do your best until the end. Maybe you have not been the perfect parent. Maybe you have done some things wrong. We all fail (Romans 3:23). However, God is able to repair mistakes and heal brokenness. Ask Him to do that for your child. Remember, God has your child covered. He is all about your child. He is for your child (Psalm 56:9).

Parenting is the toughest job I have ever had. It demands a lot, the stakes are high, the pay is minimal, and it definitely keeps the worst hours. Let's face it, the cost of parenting is great. However, the benefits far outweigh any deficiencies. There is nothing like holding a bundled baby within your arms, comforting a sick child, holding a little hand, soothing a tear, or watching your child succeed. Those are just a few of the benefits of parenting. And the cost for the lack of parenting is much greater. Society pays a high price for little ones that grow into untrained adults. Unfortunately, our world is filled with them. Nonetheless, hope remains even for those who are parentless. Isaiah 49:15 is a beautiful illustration of how God does not forget children even when the parents do not seem to care. "The Lord answers, 'Can a mother forget the baby who is nursing at her breast? Can she stop showing her tender love to the child who was born to her? She might forget her child. But I will not forget you" (NIRV).

Whether you watch your son or daughter experience their firsts, or try to protect them at every turn, the challenging road ahead is full of daily, routine tasks for parents. That does not even consider the unexpected. Detours in life do exist and they have the potential to throw your child off course. The journey around those detours can teach valuable lessons, but they must be encountered with help, *your help!*

THE STRENGTH TO STAND

As a parent or counselor, teacher or friend, where does your strength come from? Ephesians 6:10 (NIRV) says, "Finally, let the Lord make you strong. Depend on his mighty power." God will make you strong, but we must let Him do it. This is a reminder to let God be your strength. He is able. *Let Him.* "The LORD is my strength" (Exodus 15:2). Strength must be found in Christ as He is the only true source of strength. Nehemiah 8:10 offers, "The joy of the LORD is your strength." God's joy can make you strong if you ask Him for His joy. God is the source of our strength, and true joy exists only within Him. That's all good, but how do we do that? It starts by asking. Ask God for His strength. Without His strength you are likely to make only feeble attempts at parenting. So asking would be a great way to start every day.

WITHOUT HIS STRENGTH YOU ARE LIKELY TO MAKE ONLY FEEBLE ATTEMPTS AT PARENTING.

Ephesians 6:11 says, "Put on the whole armor of God, that you may be able to stand against the schemes of the devil." So you can stand and not fall. Standing is emphasized several times throughout the Bible because when you stand you are properly prepared for war. You will not fall in God's strength, but if you do, He guarantees His hand will care for you (Psalm 37:24, NIRV). While we emphasize being fully equipped with the armor of God, we must not neglect the importance of standing (1 Corinthians 16:13; Ephesians 6:11-14). I may have the best armor around, but it is useless unless I stand. You and those in your household must learn to stand.

Why is it important for a parent to stand up in Christ? When we stand for godliness, we become a protective fortress for our children to grow in. Can you imagine how safe and confident it would be to mature in that protection? But what happens if you never stand up? Your position in Christ is not compromised. However, if you are the final line of defense in your child's life, then shouldn't you be standing?

Life is a spiritual battle, and it is not against people. We are to hate evil, while learning to love people. It may be hard to remember when you are surrounded by enemies, but this fight is not against flesh and blood. It is in hopes of destroying the enemy's hold.

> *I do live in the world. But I don't fight my battles the way the people of the world do. The weapons I fight with are not the weapons the world uses. In fact, it is just the opposite. My weapons have the power of God to destroy the camps of the enemy* (2 Corinthians 10:3-4, NIRV).

There is a power within this Scripture for you. God gives you the power to take down strongholds. Variations occur from case to case, but warfare generally begins once the true enemy is identified. As Christ's soldiers, we must be properly trained to use our weapons. The goal should be helping, not hurting people. Plenty of spiritually-abused people already exist and more are not needed. Do your part to stand strong and know who the *true* enemy is.

"Take up the whole armor of God..." Ephesians 6:13 says. If you have helped your child to put her (his) trust in God, she (he) has been provided a full suit of spiritual armor. First, you are instructed to take up the armor. Does this verse imply that the armor of God can be taken off or put down? In what condition is your child's armor? Is it down? Is it tarnished? God's

USE GOD'S ARMOR TO PROTECT YOU AND YOUR CHILD.

armor is made for our protection. It acts as a protective layer against the evil of this world. Use God's armor to protect you and your child. Take it up, put it on, and protect your child. A protective covering comes through prayer. Petition God for your child's spiritual armor to be picked up, and put on.

Why is this protection so important? It offers your child the ability to withstand the attacks of this world and provides him or her with a boost of spiritual encouragement. As this truth settles within your heart, more opportunities to plant truth will arise. God will equip you for every good work even if the work ahead seems hard and filled with darkness. He will help you stand. When you stand with God, you won't just stand *you'll stand firm.*

INNOVATIVE AND HIGHLY FUNCTIONAL

So take everything the Master has set out for you, well-made weapons of the best materials… Be prepared. You're up against far more than you can handle on your own. Take all the help you can get, every weapon God has issued, so that when it's all over but the shouting you'll still be on your feet (Ephesians 6:10, 13, MSG).

Put on every piece of the armor. Do you know what that means? We all have areas where we need to grow. Don't feel like you need to have all the answers. Instead of that, continue in a constant pursuit to find answers. Wisdom and understanding start there (Proverbs 2). Begin each day by asking God what you need to do and where to start.

Ephesians 6:14 (NIV) directs us to "Stand firm." You are to stand firmly planted in the truth. In order to do so, you must know the truth. Get to know God's Word, and teach it to your family (Deuteronomy 6:7). The Word of God is also able to equip you for every spiritual battle of the mind. Applying Scripture to your life will reap benefits, including in the life of your child.

The first piece of armor is the belt of truth. Be honest and truthful with your child. While teaching a group of graduate counseling students, I asked them, "Whatever happened to being honest in counseling?" I meant it. So many of us struggle with that today. Our society is built upon lies and empty promises. We are politically correct, but not honest in how we handle one another. People long for truth, not political correctness. They can get political correctness anywhere. What they long for is the truth (Psalm 25:5, NIV). Another misconception about truth is based upon our individual perceptions. Many people base their truth upon their own perceptions, and perceptions can easily lead to deception. We lack for trust in our society. Rightfully so, but that ultimately impacts our view of truth and trusting one another. Contrary to all this, God's Word remains true. It has the ability to set people free (John 8:32). We all need a daily dose of truth, including children who can benefit from a daily allowance of God's truth. Does your child take vitamins daily? We do that to supplement any deficits within their diet. But do you give your child a daily supply of truth? Is your child getting enough? Are you willing to meet his (her) daily spiritual needs? The very supplements you and your family need are found within the truth.

I love that truth is chosen to be the belt. It is placed in the middle of your body to impact you in all directions. Truth travels from your child's head down to his (her) little toes. God's truth will affect how he thinks, what he feels, where he goes, and ultimately what he does. Truth is meant to impact his mind and entire life. Truth directs where he will go (Psalm 16:11; 119:105). In what direction is your child headed? Let the foundation of truth direct him or her.

SATAN IS AT THE HEART OF EVERY LIE.

We are instructed to buckle the belt of truth and fasten it on. Have you ever had a belt that didn't fit? A belt that is too loose does not serve its purpose. Or if it's too tight it's likely to break. The belt of truth is the same way. It needs to be properly fitted, secure, and in place. Do not let truth get away from you. Buckle it on and fasten it on your child through prayer.

Unfortunately, the father of lies, Satan, roars around desperately trying to deceive (John 8:44; 1 Peter 5:8). Satan is at the heart of every lie (Acts 5:1-11). You and your child both need to know that, so that truth will prevail.

One benefit of knowing truth is that you no longer listen to lies (1 John 4:6, NIRV). When a friend of mine was going through a horrible trial in life, she struggled. But later found that for the first time ever she was able to recognize and understand truth. It was priceless. However, the presence of truth in our lives is not without pain at times. It can be painful to know you were blind, lied to, or deceived. As a parent or therapist, you must know truth for yourself in order to train others in the ways of truth. Get to know God's truth and let it transform your walk, your talk, and your life.

A belt is literally used to keep your pants up. If your belt comes off your pants are likely to fall down, and once exposed, everything is revealed. God exposes everything to the light. "For everything that is hidden will eventually be brought into the open, and every secret will be brought to light" (Mark 4:22, NLT). Lies will not stand against the light. Hopefully that is encouraging if you have experienced betrayal and lying. In the long run, it is better to be upfront with the truth. So if you are exposed, you can stand. Basing life on truth is a better way to live. Again, there is freedom in the truth.

> *It's a scandal when people waste their lives on things they must do in darkness where no one will see. Rip the cover off those frauds and see how attractive they look in the light of Christ. Wake up from your sleep, climb out of your coffins; Christ will show you the light! So watch your step. Use your head. Make the most of every chance you get. These are desperate times!* (Ephesians 5:11-16, MSG).

Dark elements generally foster a sense of shame. Are you hiding anything from God? Talk to Him about it. Start by exposing your darkness to God's light. Then include the life of your child.

> *God is light, and in him is no darkness at all. If we say we have fellowship with him while we walk in darkness, we lie and do not practice the truth. But if we walk in the light, as he is in the light, we have fellowship with one another, and the blood of Jesus his Son cleanses us from all sin. If we say we have no sin, we deceive ourselves, and the truth is not in us* (1 John 1:5-7).

Walk in the truth, and train your child to also.

Next, we are instructed to put on the breastplate of righteousness. It is also referred to as "the armor of godliness" in Ephesians 6:14 (NIRV). In essence, righteous is being in right standing with God. This does not translate into perfection. You do not have to be perfect to have a relationship with God. But it does include being morally right, just, and blameless. On our own, none of us would be counted righteous (Romans 3:10). Thankfully, we have a Savior who makes us righteous because of who He is. Righteousness is the result of keeping short accounts with God because of Jesus. It is the daily spiritual cleansing of confessing your sins to Him. The Scriptures give an example, "I admit that I have done wrong. I am troubled by my sin" (Psalms 38:18, NIRV). It is talking to God through prayer with the desire to let nothing stand in the way of your relationship with God. On a grander scale, your breastplate shares the representation of taking up your cross daily to follow Him (Luke 9:23-25, NIV).

Your feet can walk in peace. Shoes of peace literally provide that. "Wear on your feet what will prepare you…" (Ephesians 6:15, NIRV). Preparation comes when your soul is filled with peace. Peace will prepare you. Have you ever thought about that? Life can get crazy around you. But when you have peace, you are okay. Things may not be perfect, but you are prepared when you have peace. When is the last time you or your child felt peace?

Have you ever walked in shoes that did not fit right? Ill-fitting shoes are terrible! They are uncomfortable, irritating, and can be mind-consuming. They can steal your focus and become all you think about. All the while, God offers peace, and His peace fits perfectly. "Peace I leave with you; my peace I give to you. Not as the world gives do I give to you. Let not your hearts be troubled, neither let them be afraid" (John 14:27). Philippians 4:7 states, "And the peace of God, which surpasses all understanding, will guard your hearts and your minds in Christ Jesus." If your feet are planted in peace, then the storms in life (the wind, the rain, the depression, the abuse, the economic woes, all the preeminent evil around you) cannot shake you from a posture of peace. Of course, these things will affect you. They can impact and change you. However, the difference comes in having peace of mind amidst the storm (Isaiah 26:3). Peace can be shared with others. This all can occur while you remain in His peace. So when anxieties come, and they will, you remain strong. "When the cares of my heart are many, your consolations cheer my soul" (Psalm 94:19). Do you have many cares upon your heart? A heart filled with cares can find peace. God has peace for you and your child. Are you willing to ask Him for peace?

The shield of faith is the next piece of spiritual armor. "Also, pick up the shield of faith. With it you can put out all of the flaming arrows of the evil one" (Ephesians 6:16, NIRV). Do you become worried when the enemy attacks? Ephesians 6:16 claims we have everything we need to win. We can fight all the darts of evil with faith. Victory exists here. Do you live that way when attacks come? Many of us choose to live in defeat. However, through faith there exists another route.

Matthew 17:20 offers this hope, "If you have faith like a grain of mustard seed, you will say to this mountain, 'Move from here to there,' and it will move, and nothing will be impossible for you." Have you ever seen the size of a mustard seed? It is teeny-tiny. God's hope to you is this: you do not need mammoth amounts of faith to see change. "All things are possible for one who believes" (Mark 9:23). Remember Abraham's story?

YOU DO NOT NEED MAMMOTH AMOUNTS OF FAITH TO SEE CHANGE.

Have doubts ever held you back? Or do you ever doubt God? Do you doubt His healing touch for your child? In Mark chapter nine, we find a broken-hearted father desperately seeking help for his tormented son. The father pleads with Jesus' disciples to heal him, but they cannot. Why not? Is it a faith issue? Jesus describes faith this way to the tired and frustrated dad. "Jesus said [to him], 'If? There are no "ifs" among believers. Anything can happen'" (Mark 9:23, MSG). Faith in God has the ability to move mountains and molehills in life. It also carries with it the promise to change "ifs" into belief (John 20:27, NIV).

The helmet of Salvation is next. Salvation is the act of being saved or delivered. Our deliverer, Jesus, offers salvation as a free gift. You have the opportunity to offer salvation to *this child*. Salvation is the helmet that will fit securely around his (her) mind. It offers a new way of thinking. This helmet overrules every spiritual battle we encounter. When we believe what the Scriptures say, Satan does not stand a fighting chance. Thought patterns can be transformed and minds renewed through the Word of God (Romans 12:2). Unfortunately, the world does not possess what your child needs to win this spiritual war, *but God does.* As your child learns to think upon Him, God will help him (her) win because God is able (Hebrews 12:1-2; 2 Corinthians 9:8).

The final piece of armor is the sword of the Spirit, which is the Word of God. Do you know the Word? Can you use it like a tool to defend yourself against the enemy? Can you use it on behalf of your child? That is its purpose. It's to help you through every spiritual war. For some, Bibles are nothing more than ornamental decorations that collect dust. Do you really think that is how God intended us to use this gift? Or do you view the Bible as a good source of history, but not relevant for you today? Do you really think God meant it for that purpose? Why would God create a manual, a handbook so to speak, without allowing it to supersede all generations?

Why would God have His Son become the Living Word if there was no application in it for you and I today (John 1:1-5)? If the Word of God is transforming, then why not rely more heavily upon it? God's Word does transform, but you must be willing to actively engage with it. "Blessed are those who hear God's word and obey it" (Luke 11:28, NIRV). Hear it, and then *do something* with it. Learn how to operate this sword by first applying it to yourself, then branch out and apply it to your child's life. "For the word of God is living and active, sharper than any two-edged sword, piercing to the division of soul and of spirit, of joints and of marrow, and discerning the thoughts and intentions of the heart" (Hebrews 4:12). Do you believe the Word of God has power? Do you believe His Word can slice through darkness for your child? This is unlikely to happen without belief and application.

According to John 1:14, Jesus is the Word that became flesh. How well do you know Jesus? Do you know how to grow in intimacy with Him? If not, spend time reading the book of John. It's a great place to start. Also, seek out godly wisdom in seasoned veterans of the faith.

"Let the word of Christ dwell in you richly..." (Colossians 3:16). Second Timothy 2:15 adds, "Do your best to present yourself to God as one approved, a worker who has no need to be ashamed, rightly handling the word of truth." We are accountable for how we handle the Word of God. How are you doing? You may need to evaluate yourself at times, asking, "How well am I handling God's Word?" At some point, all Christians have needed to learn the Word. We all have areas where we can improve, so the question becomes "will you?" Will you make an engaged effort to study the Bible? Utilize the Bible in the life of *this child*, and it can act as an indispensable weapon (Ephesians 6:13-18, MSG).

Finally, the armor concludes with prayer. "At all times, pray by the power of the Spirit. Pray all kinds of prayers. Be watchful, so that you can pray. Always keep on praying for all of God's people" (Ephesians 6:18, NIRV). Pray until the end, and never give up. "Prayer is essential in this ongoing warfare. Pray hard and long. Pray for your brothers and sisters. Keep your eyes open. Keep each other's spirits up so that no one falls behind or drops out" (Ephesians 6:13-18, MSG). Prayer is our opportunity to have intimate communication with a holy God. It is a powerful expression of His love toward us. God desires communication with you. Therefore, use this mighty tool with your child.

PRAYER IS OUR OPPORTUNITY TO HAVE INTIMATE COMMUNICATION WITH A HOLY GOD.

Do not let these truths fall upon you like dead weight.

Then they will not be like their ancestors—stubborn, rebellious, and unfaithful, refusing to give their hearts to God. The warriors of Ephraim, though armed with bows, turned their backs and fled on the day of battle. They did not keep God's covenant and refused to live by his instructions (Psalm 78:8-10, NLT).

These warriors of Ephraim had full armor, were ready for battle, and then they turned their backs. They did nothing. Instead of being like Ephraim's warriors, keep God's commands and apply His truth. Then the battle will begin to change.

Our boldest enemies have been plundered. They lie before us in the sleep of death. No warrior could lift a hand against us. At the blast of your breath, O God of Jacob, their horses and chariots lay still. No wonder you are greatly feared! Who can stand before you when your anger explodes? (Psalm 76:5-7, NLT).

Help your child join the winning side. Who doesn't like to win?

THE NEW STANDARD

All right soldier, yes you! Christ followers are called to be soldiers (2 Timothy 2:3). So soldier, how are you doing? Do you feel protected? Is your armor up or down? Do you even know the first thing about battle?

In the United States, the Department of Defense is made up of five branches: Air Force, Army, Coast Guard, Marine Corps, and Navy. Together, the primary missions of each entity combine to create the greatest military power on earth. The primary purpose of the Air Force and Reserve as well as the Air Force National Guard is to provide air support for the country's defense. The Army and Army Reserve are a dominant power, securing the land, guarding the assets, and instilling order and values. These men and women are considered elite warriors, dedicated to serve. The Coast Guard and Reserve provide rescue operations on the waterway, enforce maritime law, prevent harmful traffic on the waterways, and keep them clear. The Marine Corps and Reserve provide rapid-reaction to national security threats and are known as the world's fiercest warriors. The Navy and Reserve provide security and protection, while creating peace and stability on the seas.[3] All these entities combine to protect our people and to ensure the maintenance of life as normal.

Could characteristics similar to these be used to describe the body of Christ? Or you? What are the similarities between a Christian and the nation's line of defense? You have been offered the opportunity to fly, to be set apart, to be a dominant power with Christ, to be secure, to instill order and values, and to guard (Isaiah 40:31; 2 Timothy 2:21; Revelation 20:6; Proverbs 1:33; 1 Corinthians 14:40; 1 Timothy 6:20). In light of these opportunities, would you be considered an elite warrior, dedicated to serving? Are you accomplishing God's mission in your life? Are you protecting innocence and creating stability for those around you? Are you rescuing, enforcing truth, preventing destruction, or clearing the path for others (Isaiah 57:14; 61:1)? Do you provide rapid-response to those in need? I believe this should describe us as Christians.

A good soldier receives intense training to complete his or her mission. How well have you been trained? Is the world a better place just because you exist? *Is it?* Are you making a difference right where you are? We all need to be trained, and we all have the ability to impact someone. Maybe *this child* is where you need to start making a difference. You might change the world by one small step. One act of kindness, one helping hand, or one obedient heart might be all that is needed to change his (her) world.

ONE ACT OF KINDNESS, ONE HELPING HAND, OR ONE OBEDIENT HEART MIGHT BE ALL THAT IS NEEDED TO CHANGE HIS (HER) WORLD.

All branches of the military combine to accomplish a greater mission. The body of Christ is similarly created to be just that force. When humility and obedience are embraced, this unified body of believers can be powerful. What would really happen if Christians joined together in unity (Psalm 133:1, NIV)? How would our homes, schools, churches, and businesses reflect that change? We are to have one aim, it is to please God (2 Timothy 2:4). How well are you doing with that? Are you living in unity or at odds with others? Christ's soldiers are to lead the fight in forgiveness and bearing with one another (Colossians 3:13, NIV). "Soldiers don't get tied up in the affairs of civilian life, for then they cannot please the officer who enlisted them." (2 Timothy 2:4, NLT). Are you entangled in anything that needs to be addressed?

Asking God to be the final authority over your decisions will help to keep you focused (1 Kings 22:5). It pleases God when we seek Him first (Matthew 6:33). Aim to please God, and let Him instruct your pursuits. "Let your eyes look directly forward, your gaze be straight before you" (Proverbs 4:25). Allow your heart to be open to these truths so you may have purpose for every step (1 Corinthians 9:26, NLT). "And after you have done everything you can, you will still be standing" (Ephesians 6:13, NIRV).

BRING YOUR CHILD

Have you noticed what happens at political rallies? Generally, people wave signs, chant cheers, and offer their babies for a photo with the candidate or a touch from him (her). The chance that this might be the next great leader overwhelms many proud parents. Similarly, in the New Testament account, "Some people brought little children to Jesus. They wanted him to place his hands on the children and pray for them. But the disciples told the people to stop" (Matthew 19:13, NIRV). Jesus was that great leader everyone was seeking. There was no comparison. That is why adults brought children to Him.

Scripture shares that people brought the children, but it does not specify that these folks were parents. We can surmise, therefore, that today grandparents, aunts, uncles, counselors, friends, youth leaders, cousins, teachers, as well as parents may bring children to Jesus.

CHILDREN MATTER TO JESUS.

The disciples told them not to bother Jesus with children. Children were a mere distraction to the disciples. There was work that needed to be done and children got in the way. There was no time for them. Once again, Jesus would blow the disciples away. He corrected their harsh views and proud statements. Jesus poured out love. As a society today we rarely place value on the right things, much like the disciples. We tend to value things and not people, including children. However, Jesus encouraged the children to come to Him. Do not let anything stand in the way of a child seeking the Lord. Children matter to Jesus.

Adults brought children to be touched and blessed by Jesus. Who doesn't need Jesus' touch and blessing? Everyone could use a little blessing, but few receive them. Based on this Scripture, I regularly practiced a group initiative called The Blessing Circle.[4] The group gathers, forming a circle. We select one individual to stand in the middle of his or her peers. Just as Jesus brought the children in the middle of a group to bless them, this group would do likewise. Group members verbally bless the person in the middle. Everyone is given an opportunity to share what they value in this person. We conclude by praying over this individual.

This time together is priceless and has the potential to develop healing. Many adults and sometimes children have no idea how valuable they are. They may never know unless it is shared with them. Some people have experienced more curses than blessings in their lives. Therefore, The Blessing Circle offers a rare opportunity for transformation. It holds the potential to restore blessings over curses. This can be done in families or in groups. However, in group settings it works best when the group is fairly established or friendships exist among the members. I would strongly encourage you to hold The Blessing Circle for *this child*.

Jesus spent time with children. They were important to Him, and He took time to be with them. Are your children blessed when they spend time with you? Do you consider the time you have with your children valuable? Make your time together count. Show children that they have value to you. Put down your cell phone and enjoy your child for a while. Understand that what you pour into a child is likely to be reproduced later on. Therefore, spend time together and create something valuable.

Jesus understands the value and worth of children. He loves them and recognizes their importance to the future. He does not see them as a bother. Children are the future. They possess great value. They often possess greater value than we realize. Do you see children as the future? Satan fully grasps this concept. The enemy knows that training begins at birth. He wastes no time in setting up his suggestive worldview and opinions in seemingly innocent ways in the lives of young children. Hence, the power of some extreme religions and political movements. They know if they capture children early, they will likely have them for life.

"Jesus said, 'Let the little children come to me. Don't keep them away. The kingdom of heaven belongs to people like them'" (Matthew 19:14, NIRV).

> …The disciples came to Jesus and asked, 'Who is greatest in the Kingdom of Heaven?' Jesus called a little child to him and put the child among them. Then he said, 'I tell you the truth, unless you turn from your sins and become like little children, you will never get into the Kingdom of Heaven. So anyone who becomes as humble as this little child is the greatest in the Kingdom of Heaven' (Matthew 18:1-4, NLT).

Jesus welcomed children. He blessed them and offered His kingdom to them. People may say, "Oh, it's just a child." But Jesus answers, "No, this is my child. Let him come to me." God feels that very same way about every child, including yours.

RUN WITHOUT COMPROMISE

The road ahead of you may not be an easy one. Actively pursuing anyone involves challenges and risks. So, there are a few issues to consider as you become involved in the life of *this child*. First, kids need to know that you care. They need to understand that your concern is authentic and that you are worthy of their trust. Children are resilient. However, they may still resist your attempts to join in their life at least initially. Be honest with kids and tell them up front your purpose in pursuing them. Remember, children are different from adults. They generally lack adult defenses and cognitive abilities. However, what they may lack in insight they greatly make up for with imagination.[5]

It's difficult to make generalizations about any of the populations we will address. However, some lines are drawn in order to establish workable treatment strategies. A child exhibiting impulsive behaviors might act in one way, while an anxiety-ridden child may act in an entirely different way, although they both may share some of the same characteristics. Not every element may apply to every label, but it does offer a starting place.

In the social and emotional worlds problems can be compounding. "When it rains, it pours," as the saying goes. Someone who struggles with one of these areas is likely to have coexisting symptoms in another area. Therefore, it would be wise to review each book in this series individually for the sheer fact that similarities and intersects may occur. As this journey begins, be prepared to daily pick up the matters of concern involving *this child*.

CHAPTER 3
IMPULSIVE BEHAVIOR

Attention Deficit Hyperactivity Disorder, otherwise known as ADHD, is the most commonly diagnosed disorder among children and adolescents. Sadly if your child has it, you know it, and so do most of the folks around you. Children exhibiting ADHD symptoms are "more active, restless, and fidgety than typical children."[6] They tend to show significant problems in complying with adult commands, have difficulty following instructions in the absence of an instructor, and struggle with delayed gratification or resisting temptation. Lacking self-control, having difficulty adhering to rules and regulations, and trouble adapting to their environments are common symptoms of this developmental disorder.[7] Understandably, parents of these kids report higher than average degrees of stress.[8]

One treatment strategy for impulsive behaviors includes the use of stimulation delays that allow the child time to stop and think. A "Stop and Think" paper is a manipulative strategy created by teachers and clinicians that creates a window of time for the child to process successfully before responding to his (her) environment. The goal of a Stop and Think paper is to allow the child time to establish and think of positive responses, and then hopefully make the right choice. Stop and Think papers can be found online or by contacting your local school. With or without this method, give your child detailed instructions about appropriate behaviors to enhance positive choices.

At first, training your child to stop and think may seem like boot camp. Other days may be more like a dance between you and a partner who frequently steps on your toes. But this is geared to help your child mature.

Clinicians have also found repetition to be useful with ADHD sufferers. Other treatment strategies include creating realistic goals and objectives with the child, avoiding power struggles, trying behavior modification, and pursuing social skills training. Parents and therapists alike have found it helpful to use lots of external cues (notes or reminders). The integration of various learning strategies has also been beneficial for some households with struggling learners (e.g. Right Brain learning).

While some believe that food elimination diets improve the abilities of the child, others have found stimulant medications, antidepressants, and antihypertensives to be vital in their ADHD treatment.

The one piece of this developmental battle that we will tackle is impulsivity. For the purpose of this study, we will explore the life of Simon Peter, brother of Andrew, and one of Jesus' disciples. References from this point forward will refer specifically to males. Males and females alike may struggle with impulsive behaviors. However, a higher rate of occurrence is reported among the male population. Nonetheless, this material may easily be adapted to address females who also experience impulsive behaviors.

IMPULSIVE PETER

Who is "Impulsive Peter?" Some might characterize an impulsive child as quick on the draw, full of exaggerations, careless with words, lacking in discernment and follow-through. Even if you don't have a Peter in your own family, you very likely have met one. These kids react without thinking. In a disagreement, they are usually the first to strike, and generally need to get the last word in. If football were the game of life, then impulsive children would constantly be guilty of being off-sides. All of this appears to be true of the biblical Peter. He was often the first to speak, exaggerated details, denied the truth, was quick to defend, and leapt over obstacles in a single bound. Peter was a passionate man. In Matthew 26:33 (NIRV) he told Jesus, "All the others may turn away because of you. But I *never* will" (emphasis added). However later on, Peter would repeatedly deny knowing Jesus. He had charisma, and he got caught up in the moment on more than one occasion.

A trusted friend to Jesus, Peter is the one who will cut off a man's ear to protect Jesus, and deny knowing Him all within a few hours of time. But he is also the only disciple to walk on water and is first out of the boat when Jesus returns. In exploring his life, we will search for the good qualities within impulsiveness.

Who is Peter? The Bible tells us with the mere meaning of his name. It is interesting that Jesus' first interactions referred to Peter mainly as Simon. Simon means, "listening"[9] or "He who hears."[10] It's as if Jesus were saying, "Simon Peter, are you listening?" Your "Peter," if you will, may also need constant reminders of, "Hey, are you listening?" Over-learning is a key technique with impulsive children.

Keep in mind, there is hope. One day Simon Peter would transition from a daily struggle of listening into the "rock" (Matthew 16:18). There is meaning to his name (John 1:42, NIRV). Literally translated Peter means the rock.[11] No longer questioning, "Simon, are you listening?" Peter finally matures, settles into his abilities, and completes the work prepared for him. For the use of this study "Impulsive Peter" will represent anyone struggling with impulsive characteristics, all the while brimming with hope, promise, and internal ambition.

THE BOLDNESS OF PETER

Emphasize your Peter's positives, and train him to think biblical thoughts about himself. What does that mean? While we recognize Peter's impulsiveness, we also need to acknowledge his ability to be bold. This was one of Peter's most valuable and dangerous assets. Peter had boldness, and his boldness was used for Jesus. In Acts 4:29 Peter prayed and asked for an increase in boldness, "Help us to be very bold when we speak your word" (NIRV). Pray for your child to be bold and to use his boldness for God. Peter was helpful to the body. Pray that your child is helpful, too, and not hurtful with boldness. Your job is not to tell "Impulsive Peter" that he is wrong as much as it is to help him filter through the impulses to demonstrate and exemplify useful behavior.

Peter used his impulsive behavior to defend the Lord and His cause. Could we be that bold? Called before the Jewish religious leaders for their preaching about Jesus, Peter and his companion were bold. "But Peter and John replied 'Judge for yourselves. Which is right from God's point of view? Should we obey you? Or God? There's nothing else we can do. We have to speak about the things we've seen and heard'" (Acts 4:19-20, NIRV). This is an instance where Peter's impulsiveness is used for good. God is always capable of using our mess-ups, hang-ups, and mix-ups for good just as He did for Peter (Romans 8:28).

When called, Peter immediately followed Jesus (Matthew 4:18-20, NIRV). Put an impulsive child in a room of kids, and tell them it's time to meet a superstar athlete. Guess who is first in line, jumping up and down, waving his arms? Call an impulsive child to something that engages his attention and *he will come!* However, pay attention to how you call him. What tone of voice are you using with your Impulsive Peter? How are you calling him? Does the sound of your voice make him want to come or flee? Remember Peter is impulsive, but he will come to the right call. When Peter's attention is captured, he will immediately follow. When he is not engaged, repetition may be necessary. However, set limits with your child. Understand that he may need warnings. Allow for those, but also

> **WHEN PETER'S ATTENTION IS CAPTURED, HE WILL IMMEDIATELY FOLLOW.**

implement limits and boundaries. Forewarn him and then warn him a designated number of times. Remember, Simon Peter, are you listening?

Andrew, Peter's brother, brought him to Jesus (John 1:40-42, NIRV). Someone close to Peter, brought him to Jesus. He did not go on his own. Someone he trusted brought him. Peter was bold, but it took someone else to get him to Jesus. Keep this in mind, anytime you send your impulsive child to try new things. Andrew took Peter. Your Peter might be at his best when someone he trusts is on hand. Send your child with an Andrew when he explores things for the first few times. Furthermore, who is willing to take your child to Jesus?

THE GIFT OF IMPULSIVENESS

Peter scolds Jesus. Oh, for real? Yes, he actually did (Matthew 16:22, NIRV)! Our impulsive man, Peter, does the unimaginable. He gives grief to Jesus! We look at that and chuckle. We think, "Oh, I could see my impulsive child doing that." But don't laugh too quickly! There may have been a time you acted in a similar way. Have you ever gone to God angered by injustice, broken promises, death, or with shattered dreams? Have you ever demanded an explanation from God or requested a refund for your pain? We grin and think, "Oh, my child would do that!" While generally, the finger remains pointing back at us. Even pious demands and painful self-pity can result in a wedge of anger between you and God. Think for a moment; have you ever told Jesus what to do? Do not be quick to judge your child until you give a thoughtful response (Romans 2:1). Nonetheless, Peter did do the unimaginable. He scolded Jesus.

How does Jesus handle Peter's reproach? Jesus rebukes Peter's words, but he never rebukes Peter as a person. Peter rebukes God's Son, and God sets him straight. It's as if He was saying, "These thoughts are not my ways. Come on, Peter, get in agreement with me and what I have to say." In Mark 8:33 (NIRV) Jesus describes it this way. "You are not thinking about the things of God. Instead, you are thinking about human things." Train your impulsive Peter in God's thoughts toward himself, and in God's ways, not with mere human thoughts. Get him to think upon God's thoughts (Philippians 4:8). Set him straight as Jesus did and watch him begin to soar to new heights. As you do this, remember all things take time to grow whether we like it or not.

Only a few verses earlier, Jesus commissioned Peter for his future. Jesus said, "Here is what I tell you. You are Peter. On this rock I will build my church. The gates of hell will not be strong enough to destroy it" (Matthew 16:18-19, NIRV). Did you hear that? The gates of hell would not prevail over what God had in store for Peter. His plans and purposes would carry through. They do for each one of us, too. Rest assured, one day Peter also reached his destination.

Did immaturity hold Peter back? That's a good question. Each one of us is to be developing and maturing. The hope is that progress is occurring for all of us (Hebrews 5:11-14, NIV). Sometimes when a child possesses an impulsive nature, immaturity attempts to hang on as long as possible. It can present itself in foolish ways. You will need keys to work with immature behavior. How has God equipped your Peter? It will be important for you to answer that question for Peter's growth. Pray. Asking for godly insight into your Peter's immature heart.

Remember the disciple Peter is the very same guy who had just told Jesus He was wrong. Like you have never done that before, right? Like you have never faced adversity and questioned, "What in the world is going on?" The same is true of Peter, and God still did incredible things through him.

Six days later, Jesus took Peter, James, and John to the mountaintop with him (Matthew 17:1). In the midst of God's amazing plan, Peter got a break. Why wait? Why did Jesus wait six days after Peter made a mistake? Was it, perhaps, because Peter needed a break, and Jesus knew it? Peter needed to comprehend his mistake, repent, and then soak in the grace of Jesus. Peter probably needed frequent breaks. Just like your Peter probably does.

Two lessons may be helpful from these events. First, Peter may have needed a break after being reprimanded by the Lord. Like it or not, he probably felt that way. Second, Peter needed to see a positive side to this situation. A getaway, a mountaintop experience is exactly what any Peter would need following a time of discipline. This is a useful time for healing, especially when it includes time with the Lord. So, it's not difficult to deduce that Peter did need breaks. Peter needed some time following a reprimand. But Peter also desperately needs a positive mountaintop experience, whether he succeeds or fails. Think of your own situation. When you have failed or been stressed to the max, don't you long to get away and to be refreshed? Do you long for a highlight? We all do. These mountaintop experiences were based on who Peter was as a person, not upon what he did. Jesus still took Peter to the mountaintop with Him simply because Peter belonged. What mountaintop experiences have you provided for your Peter? Are you planning any? Jesus did. He understood that they were needed.

We all mess up daily (Romans 3:23, NIV). Because of that, we need breaks, time alone with God, and mountaintop experiences built into our lives. What happens with most impulsive kids is that they get plenty of punishments automatically. Usually no one has a problem punishing Peters. However, we tend to lack in the positives with these kids. Quite frankly, most Peters share this in common. They have a long list of negatives that easily become the focus. If you focus only on the negatives with Peter, he will never get past his failures. Who wants their child stuck in failures? Peter desperately needs *mountaintops to win.*

IMPULSIVENESS CAN BE GOOD.

Peter is brave enough to speak the truth, and he knows his stuff (Mark 8:29, NIRV). Another of Peter's great attributes is that he knows his personal tastes; and the things he likes, he knows well. Biblical Peter's impulsiveness could have constantly worked positively, promoting God. *Impulsiveness can be good.* But your Peter needs to learn to utilize it when it is appropriate. What are the things your Peter knows about? What are his interests? He is likely to be an expert in something. Start there. Then figure out when impulsiveness might be useful for your Peter. Seek wisdom as you explore the benefits of impulsiveness in your child's life.

An impulsive response rushes one's heart. That rush may simultaneously manifest itself with the physical symptoms of increased adrenaline, an acceleration of the heart, sweaty palms, clinched fists, or a tightened jaw. Peter may have experienced similar symptoms before cutting off the servant's ear. If nothing else, help your Peter understand this. Young Peter needs to understand that God generally will not rush him. In His Word, God often refers to waiting upon Him. Most of the time, the rushing sensation that quickly consumes impulsive natures, has nothing to do with God and can be stopped. But first, Peter needs to identify the source of that sensation, and the source is generally not the Lord. That's not to say that sometimes the Lord will not move quickly. But if young Peters know that those urges many times do not come from God, then they might possibly be controlled.

Hang around counseling offices long enough, and you will probably hear the term "impulse control" mentioned. Impulse control is the ability to identify consuming thoughts and to control them before they lead to poor responses. Would Peter have cut off the soldier's ear had he used impulse control? Probably not. But at that time, Peter did not understand. Help your child understand the source that causes him to rush. This will help foster lasting impulse control.

Peter does not give up. He is determined and persistent. Peter is even forcefully persistent with Jesus (Mark 14:31). I love this about Peter! What Peter lacks in follow-through, he makes up for with persistence. Peter does not see obstacles or roadblocks. His eye is on the prize and he is confident he can do it. This is Peter's impulsiveness at its best!

BE REAL WITH PETER

Your Peter will need warnings. Jesus gave fair warnings to Peter. In Matthew 26:34 Jesus says to him, "'It will happen this very night. Before the rooster crows, you will say three times that you don't know me'" (NIRV). Peter followed with the typical Peter response. "Huh, me? No way, Lord. You have the wrong guy." In reality, Peter is more dramatic than that. Peter says, "I may have to die with you. But I will never say I don't know you" (Matthew 26:35, NIRV). Don't think for a moment that Peter was alone in that pledge. He was not. The others all agreed with him. But once again, Peter is willing to speak his mind.

Nonetheless, the point is that your Peter will need warnings. He needs to be told in ample enough time that failure is a possibility, and at the same time he needs to be reminded that he is thoroughly loved despite the outcome. Lay out the rules for Peter. Do any necessary groundwork ahead of time for him because he won't be able to. Tell Peter the plans especially as it relates to school. You may need to do it several times. Warning and directing Peter before an event may be a lifesaver and a necessary preparation tool for your family.

Tell Peter the truth. If there is one thing that Peter longs for, it's the truth. He may not always agree, but he can handle truth. Peter *needs truth.*

Simon Peter was also observant of his surroundings. He was the first to notice the fig tree Jesus had cursed. With astonishment Peter says, "Rabbi, look! The fig tree you put a curse on has dried up!" (NIRV). Peter watched Jesus and remembered. Impulsive eyes are all around us, observing actions and internalizing behaviors. They will remember the good and the bad. Here is the challenge to you parents: Peter's eyes are watching. Be careful what you curse or refer to negatively in front of your Peter. Remember, God has a forgiving heart if you have made mistakes.

While Peter continued to state the obvious, he also remained a man eager to hear himself speak. The progressive filter that keeps most people from sharing every thought aloud does not function in the same way for most Peters. The ability to communicate gives people a means of influence, but must be balanced to control their behavior. Some clinicians believe that internalized self-talk needs to be fully developed to establish greater control over behavior. Without the development of this progressive step, Peter may continue stating every obvious detail until his internal functioning self-speech is developed.[12]

For example, on one occasion Jesus knew that someone had touched him and that power had been released from Him. Luke 8:45 says, "They all said they didn't do it. Then Peter said,

'Master, the people are crowding and pushing against you'"
(NIRV). Peter missed the point. Jesus knew what had happened.
How often does your child miss the point like Peter? Is he
focused on the obvious, when that's obviously not the point?
Jesus was in a large crowd, and it was evident that people were
crowding around Him. But in the midst of chaos, someone
unseen seemed to have captured Jesus' power. Peter's eyes were
focused only on what could be seen (2 Corinthians 4:18).
Greater vision looks beyond trivial occurrences and focuses on
the big picture. Peter's internalized speech was not functioning
properly. Keep that in mind when your child speaks. Encourage
him to think before he responds. Repeatedly remind him to
take time to think through situations. As mentioned before,
reminder cues may be needed and are often utilized with Peters.

Mark 9:6 notes, "Peter didn't really know what to say, because
they were so afraid" (NIRV). Impulsive Peter often spoke out
of fear. Even when he was not sure what to say, he seemed
to use his words to fill up space. Your Peter will talk. He is a
talker by nature; most impulsive people are.

Peter may have lacked some character qualities, but he could
be trusted. He always remained someone Jesus trusted. Jesus
could be real with Peter (Mark 14:33-34, NIRV). Peter was a
part of Jesus' inner circle, his close group of friends. Jesus could
be Himself within this safe community. He could let down His
guard and grieve. Peter was one that Jesus trusted.
Ironically, this trusted companion of Jesus also lied. Take a look
at Peter's response when he was questioned about knowing
Jesus. "I don't know or understand what you're talking about,"

he said (Mark 14:68, NIRV). Really? Is it really that he didn't know or understand? Or was it more about protecting himself from consequences, shame, or embarrassment?

Do not assume that your impulsive child is always lying. But know that sometimes biblical Peter did lie. Impulsiveness can be a gateway to lying. Peter was afraid. He quickly reacted, and chose to lie. His boldness had dwindled to denying his friend three times. Nonetheless, don't be too quick to give up on Peter. Could you stand before God on Judgment Day and say you have never told a lie? Despite Peter's love for truth, honesty did not develop easily within him. It simply came as Peter matured, but it came at the price of denying Jesus. Do not accept lying. There were consequences for Peter's behavior. Pray your Peter matures, while showing him the value of speaking truth.

Let's take another step. Did Peter see the disappointment in Jesus' eyes after he denied knowing Him (Luke 22:61)? There was hurt, and Peter left disgraced. But, as John records the story, Jesus lovingly reinstated Peter in a repeated act of mercy. Jesus verbally pursued Peter to repent and then publicly recommitted His love for him. Knowingly or not at the time, Peter makes a verbal commitment. This time Peter used his words wisely. Confrontations are tough. No one enjoys conflict. But if Jesus was going to love Peter well, He had to pursue him at that point. Peter may have felt discouraged. Maybe he felt it was a reprimand. However, Jesus continued to pursue him to the point of being uncomfortable (John 21:15-17). Your Peter may need pursuing after he has done something wrong. But the repeated acts of mercy must be done in love. The disciple Peter needed forgiveness extended to him, mercy that followed, and grace to re-up one more time. In the end, this pursuit was used to validate Peter's allegiance, and Peter *rocked* after that pursuit. Peter and Judas, who betrayed Christ, were both fallen men. They both failed Jesus miserably. But the obvious difference is that Judas gave up and did not receive forgiveness. While Peter, on the other hand, fell often, asked for forgiveness, and *repeatedly got back up.* Peter would look defeat in the eye, get up with determination, and shout, "I will not give up!" Teach your child to run with purpose like Jesus taught Peter. Do not let your child fight aimlessly, but with understanding and with purpose (1 Corinthians 9:26, NLT).

It is important for Peter to believe; he needed faith to believe so he could do great things. Your Peter will be drawn to believe in

FREEDOM ESTABLISHES ITSELF WHEN BELIEF AND FORGIVENESS UNITE AS ONE.

something. Where will you let him be led? We, like Peter, need to believe in order to receive (John 3:16). Do you see where this is going? Peter had to believe and learn to forgive as he matured. There is no other way. In order to go forward, Peter had to forgive (Matthew 6:12; Matthew 18:22). Freedom establishes itself when belief and forgiveness unite as one. All Peters need to understand this truth.

PERSISTENT ENOUGH TO CONQUER

Many of Peter's attempts to hit the bull's-eye in life would fail drastically. Eventually though, he would hit the target. Peter possessed a persistent itch. It's his persistence that gave him fire and helped him win.

We know Peter denied knowing Jesus (Luke 22:60-61). Can you image what it was like for him to deny knowing the man he left everything for? Peter risked everything for Jesus. He abandoned his business and financial future, and then sojourned freely with Jesus. There is no financial planner that would recommend this strategy. However, Peter remained passionate for Jesus and defended him with everything that he had (John 18:10). Yet he still failed. He still sinned. The worst of it is, Jesus knew. He saw. Jesus always sees all our sin (1 John 1:5-10; Psalm 139:7-12).

Peter was not comfortable with his sin or with himself at the time. The Word of God says, "Then he began to invoke a curse on himself and to swear…" (Matthew 26:74). Anyone calling down curses upon himself is not sending out a positive vibe. How would you feel if you were Peter? Has your Peter ever felt the same way or been ashamed? Ask for healing over those specific moments because we all fail sometimes (Psalm 147:3). Bear in mind, it only took a look from Jesus for Peter to break down (Luke 22:62). A timely glance may be enough to produce a repentant heart within your Peter. You know the look! For a short time Peter was broken, but he would later return empowered. In the end, his faith would not fail him. When Peter was down, he got back up again and *he ran*.

Peter liked running. His impulsive drive was the motivating force behind most of it, but he did run a lot. Peter did not always get there first, but he was always willing to go the distance (John 20:3-10). Inhibitions did not hold him back. He did not have them. Frankly he did not need them, especially when he was going to find Jesus. So in Peter-like-fashion, he ran! It is important to note that your Peter may not finish first. *But as longs as he runs, he wins.* Because eventually Peter's impulsiveness would lead him to be the first to go in and discover that Jesus was gone from the tomb. *There is no stopping a running Peter!*

Running may be a healthy outlet for your Peter. It allows time to process, while expending physical energy to help him blow off steam. Both are great tools to utilize with an impulsive child. Also keep in mind, emotional-running usually represents key behaviors in mental health. Generally speaking, we are all running toward someone or something. Who is your Peter running toward? Know what your child is running for. What are his goals? Where does he see himself going? Remember, Peter has a need for purpose in every step (1 Corinthians 9:26). But at the same time, also be aware of what your Peter may be running from? Running can also be a sign of escape. However you shake it, running seems to be a theme with Peter.

In the end, Peter's impulsiveness would throw him overboard for Jesus. Peter literally threw himself into the sea when he saw Jesus upon the shore (John 21:3-8). *He is so impulsive!* He is so excitable! He cannot wait to see Jesus. He was not going to wait on a boat to get him there. He was not going to wait on anyone or anything. He was not waiting. He was going. In fact when the others looked around, *he was gone!*

CHAPTER 4

A DAY IN THE LIFE OF PETER

Peter's actions and their consequences

Peter is a lot of work. He is! If you have a Peter, take a bow. You deserve it! Peter can try you. He will consume endless effort and energy. But oh, the precious reward of a maturing Peter is priceless! Keep working! *Peters are worth it!* Let's look at a day in the life of Peter. What is it like to be Peter? We'll journey into Peter's walk, his world, and his wanderings.

THE INCREDIBLE ACTS OF PETER

Peter is the first named in Jesus' line-up, and he is comfortable and friendly with Jesus (Matthew 10:2; Matthew 8:14). Peter knew who he was serving (Mark 8:27-30). Do you know who your child is serving? Does he? Some impulsive kids could not tell you who they are serving, however, most generally understand their own actions. In general, they know what their behaviors will get them. In essence, they know how their behaviors serve them. Do you? Do you know what results from your Peter's behaviors? Do you know what he gets from those behaviors? Ask yourself, "Who is my child serving, and what is he getting from this?"

Matthew 14:22-32 records the details of an incredible act of Peter. Here we find Peter walking on water. Can you imagine the impulsive child saying, "Hey, I want to do that? Lord, call on me! I want to walk on water, too!" Every impulsive kid out there would be hanging over the edge, shouting, "Hey, let me in! I want to do that!" Let's face it, most of them would not wait to ask. The possibilities of sinking or swimming would never have crossed their minds. They would not have had time to process that thought because *they would already be overboard!*

Walking on water might represent various experiences in life. For your child, walking on water may represent a step of faith to trust you with his heart. Or maybe it's trusting school officials to implement a behavior plan one more time. Or maybe it's one last attempt to be himself in the midst of criticism at school.

IF INCLUSION MEANS BEING CLOSELY CONNECTED WITH YOU OR TO A BODY OF GOOD FRIENDS, THEN START THERE.

Do you feel like your child is trying to walk only to find himself drowning? Is he being pulled into the social current in society? Spend time facing any difficulties with Peter before he sinks. Remember, a little faith can keep Peter's head above water. However if he does start to sink, you can call upon Jesus. He will be right there (Matthew 28:20).

Peter was usually in close proximity to Jesus. He did not want Jesus to get too far away. Do not let your Peter get too far away either. It is great that Peter wanted to be close to Jesus. This would be helpful for every Peter. Keep him close whether he believes in Jesus or not.

Peter wants to be included. If inclusion means being closely connected with you or to a body of good friends, then start there. Peter longs to be a part of the inner circle, and he fits there. He wants in *even if he has to watch from a distance*. No matter the outcome, he will be tracking closely behind. Peter was a passionate guy. As soldiers began to fill the garden where Jesus prayed, confrontation and betrayal sparked. "Peter, having a sword, drew it and struck the high priest's servant and cut off his right ear" (John 18:10). Wait a minute, who gave the impulsive kid a weapon anyway? What impulsive person do you know that should handle a weapon? Can you just see it now? The headline in the next day's newspaper reading, "Impulsive Disciple Does Ear Piercings for Free!" Peter was probably thinking he was merely defending his Lord. Peter was as passionate as he was impulsive. Those two characteristics existed in him simultaneously and created a beautiful and dangerous combination. Left unchecked, someone could get hurt.

Jesus responded to Peter as he always did. "Put your sword away" (John 18:11, NIRV). In Luke 22:51 Jesus declared, "No more of this!" Jesus gave Peter firm instruction, repaired the damage, and continued on with His mission. Jesus fixed the damage by healing the wounded soldier's ear. Peter's errors can be distracting. They can cause those around him to lose focus. Peter acted out of ignorance as well as out of love. He acted like most impulsive Peters I know; he saw someone he cared about being threatened and he took action. What does your Peter care about enough to defend? This will be key to understanding your impulsive Peter's behaviors and motivation. Once you know the motivation, then you can create plans to prevent future damage. When Peter messes up, and he will, give firm instruction, repair the damage, and get back to work.

Peter made an impulsive mistake. He had a sword. Of course, he would defend his Lord, the one he loved. We know as his story progressed, he would deliberately make yet another costly mistake by denying the Lord he loved (John 18:15-27). Ultimately, sin would win. There is a distinct difference between these two scenarios. Can you identify it? One was a preoccupation with Peter's agenda. The other was a deliberate and absolute abandonment of Jesus. Although both acts were intentional, the former was done in passionate innocence. As a parent, a counselor, a grandparent, or a friend, it should be your goal to know the difference between these two instances. You may not know the motivation, but you will know the effect. If you lack understanding in Peter's thought processes, then ask God for understanding. Jesus obviously knew the difference between the two.

If you want to equip your kids with weapons, start with the ones that pack a spiritual punch. Train impulsive children thoroughly in the Word of God, also referred to as the sword of the Spirit (Ephesians 6:17). It is active and sharp (Hebrews 4:12). What impulsive child wouldn't like knowing that he has a spiritual sword within his grasp? What little one wouldn't gravitate toward that? If you are going to train impulsive children in something, than train them in how to use their biblical swords. What does that mean? Train them to create biblical thought patterns regarding themselves and circumstances to fight off their enemies. Use the Bible as a

WHEN PROPERLY TRAINED, YOUR PETER CAN MAKE A GREAT IMPACT SPIRITUALLY.

manual to train Peter. This truly is the safest form of weapon control.

Kids with impulsive natures need to be trained when it is appropriate to fight. Impulsive kids are not afraid to battle, but they need to understand how to battle. We each battle daily. So training for your Peter will be necessary. Answer the what, when, where, and why questions regarding your Peter's battles. Peter is worth defending. But understanding that every battle is really a spiritual battle will bring your Peter the greatest victory.

Your child must know how to defensively fight spiritual battles. How much training have you given him? Where do you start? Start by asking God. Then teach your child to pray before he responds (Proverbs 22:6). After that, train your Peter in the fruit of the Spirit and the armor of God (Galatians 5:22-23; Ephesians 6:10-18). God calls each of us to turn the other cheek (Matthew 5:39). Nonetheless, the nature of impulsive children needs to be considered as they confront battles. My wish is that all kids would turn away, but that's not reality. Therefore, equip him with every spiritual tool possible in hopes that he will remember. Then remind him to stop and pray throughout the day.

Ask God, and then detail situations where your Peter has struggled in the past. Provide alternatives and ask for wisdom

(James 1:5). Remind Peter that he is facing a different kind of battle, and his spiritual enemies may not be seen. When properly trained, your Peter can make a great impact spiritually (Ephesians 6:12; 2 Corinthians 10:3-6; Matthew 5:43-48; Romans 12:20).

Peter's instant, impulsive response caused someone else to be injured. Has your Peter ever done that? Has someone ever been hurt because your Peter rapidly responded with anger? The injury does not have to be physical. It could be emotional as well. Or have you quickly responded to your Peter and injured his heart? When is the last time you impulsively responded and hurt another person? Peter has, and you probably have as well. Most of us are guilty of that. Have you asked Jesus to heal that incident and that person? If not, now would be the best time to do it. Jesus healed the servant's ear instantly. Linger with that thought.

By the time we reach the book of Acts, Peter is a changed man in the eyes of the public. "So people brought those who were sick into the streets. They placed them on beds and mats. They hoped that at least Peter's shadow might fall on some of them as he walked by" (Acts 5:15, NIRV). Hang on, parents of impulsive children and adolescents! It may be difficult to see through your Peter's mistakes, but hang in there. Eventually, people wanted what Peter had. Jesus encouraged the positives within Peter. In the end, people actually even wanted Peter's shadow to touch them. Peter had changed, and others wanted what he had.

NOT AFRAID TO ASK

No question is left unasked when Peter is present. He is able to ask all the tough questions and offers fly-by-the-seat-of-your-pants remedies. Here is an example of Peter's impulsiveness at work (Matthew 17:24-27). The tax collectors come to Peter and say, "Hey, doesn't your Jesus pay taxes?" Peter without thinking and with no hesitation says, "Ah... Yea sure, he does." Now what has Peter done? His impulsive counter was completely inaccurate. He quickly responded and lied. He never checked out the facts. He just replied. Peter got himself into a predicament again and made matters worse by lying. All the while he is probably wondering, "How am I going to come up with the money for myself and for Jesus?"

Jesus is so cool! Instead of putting Peter in his place or making him feel ashamed, Jesus addresses the problem directly with Peter. Jesus acts before Peter even has time to speak. Jesus does not shame him for his mistakes. He does not even allow time for Peter to create additional problems. Jesus is straight forward and to the point with Peter, clearing the air with him once again. Ever been in a situation where the tension is thick and your heart is racing out-of-control? Jesus eliminates all of that here. He confronts problems directly with Peter and gets right to the heart. Do not beat around the bush with your impulsive Peter. Give him the facts, and *get to the point.*

DO NOT BEAT AROUND THE BUSH WITH YOUR IMPULSIVE PETER.

First things first, Jesus addresses the problem with Peter. He does not interrogate Peter with questions He already knows the answers to. He does not get involved in a power struggle with him. Jesus gets right to the point. "Peter, I'm God's Son, and I do not pay taxes." *Disciplining Peter begins with presenting the truth in his circumstances, and follows with fixing the problem.* Again Jesus is so cool because He uses Peter's skills to fix the problem. Peter's craft is fishing, and Jesus uses Peter's skill-set to pay for the mistake.

What skills does your Peter have? Have you ever utilized his skills for retribution? Jesus did. Belittling or becoming upset with Peter will not solve the problems. His predicaments are far too complex for that to be beneficial. Solving Peter's dilemmas means creating plans to prevent and replenish when mistakes occur. Jesus uses Peter's skill to redeem Peter's mistake. Again I ask, what is your Peter good at? Every person has a gift, so does your Peter! He has to. You may need to search for it. But do not worry because when you seek, you will find (Matthew 7:8). Use Peter's skills the next time he makes a mistake.

Biblical Peter did not have all the answers; he had to ask questions to gain insight. Your Peter may also need to ask questions and not be embarrassed. Asking questions gets your Peter one step closer to gaining knowledge that he did not have. Generally, impulsive people are willing to speak out and ask questions. Inhibitions rarely hinder them. That can be a great quality. When you lack knowledge and seek it by asking questions, you are utilizing great problem-solving skills. Encourage that with your Peter.

What Peter lacks in some areas, he makes up for with his ability to speak truth. He is not afraid to ask questions or to inquire about details that others merely wonder about. Peter never hesitates when it comes to asking, and that can be a good thing. Peter is the disciple who asked how many times he needed to forgive (Matthew 18:21-22). He wanted to be released from granting mercy until he received his own lesson on forgiveness (John 21:15-18). Pray that your Peter learns to forgive. Offering forgiveness can be challenging. It's easy to want to throw in the towel. But growth happens when forgiveness occurs. Help your Peter choose the path to forgiveness.

Peter is authentic and real. He's willing to put himself out there again and again. Peter was the only disciple brave enough to ask about rewards, while they all wanted to know. Once again, it was Peter who asked, "We have left everything to follow you! What reward will be given to us?" (Matthew 19:27, NIRV). Every eye in that place was probably fixed on Jesus. All the disciples would have wanted to know Jesus' response, but Peter was the only one willing to ask.

What is your Peter asking about these days? Listen carefully because he is probably asking some good questions. Be sure to listen for the question most Peters are asking, "What's in it for me? What is the reward?" This is why building positives into Peter and using his skill set are essential tools for constructing and capturing Peter's attention (and his heart). Peter is bright enough to know the cost and egotistic enough to seek the reward. Remember, he's probably looking for what's in it for him.

IF YOU KNOW A PETER, THEN YOU KNOW HE CAN TALK, AND TALK, AND TALK.

It may not be difficult to imagine, but as the story continues, *Peter continues talking!* This time Peter talks about making sleeping arrangements for Jesus and His crew on a mountaintop. But Jesus had other plans. The Bible says, "While Peter was still speaking..." (Matthew 17:5, NIRV). *While Peter was still speaking, God continues on with His plan.* If you know a Peter, then you know he can talk, and talk, and talk. Peters can talk their little lives away. "While Peter was still speaking." Keep that in mind. Peter will talk. He may talk your ear off. Remember, God created Peter that way. But God did not stop acting because Peter was talking. No, God proceeded with business as usual. He went right on completing all that needed to be done while Peter kept talking. You may also need to do the same thing. Carry on, proceed as normal, and complete what is necessary. Meanwhile, Peter may still be talking.

Peter matured during tough teachings by Jesus. Many people found Jesus' statements to be challenging when it came to following God. In fact, many found them to be too challenging. The Bible gives this perspective, "From this time on, many of his disciples turned back. They no longer followed him" (John 6:66, NIRV). Jesus also asked his disciples if they wanted to leave. Peter's response was invaluable, "Lord, who can we go to? You have the words of eternal life. We believe and know that you are the Holy One of God" (John

6:68-69, NIRV). Peter was growing during the challenge. Your Peter may also mature during times of challenge. Challenges are just that. They do not look fun and usually are not easy. But your Peter is likely to grow in the challenge.

Show God in tangible ways to your Peter because God's Word can transform him. The Word brought life to Peter, and he believed. *Give life to your Peter.* Train him in God's Word so he can also follow. Peter was passionate, and he served his God with that same passion.

PETER WAS PASSIONATE, AND HE SERVED HIS GOD WITH THAT SAME PASSION.

Surprising as it may be, impulsive Peter is not patient. When Jesus was talking about his betrayal, Peter wanted to have answers. He wanted the lowdown, and he wanted it now! Can you imagine Peter assessing the situation and trying to figure it out? Peter needed to be in-the-know. If Peter cannot find out the answers himself, then he will most certainly find someone else who can. So Peter whispered to John, "Hey, you ask which one of us will betray him" (John 13:24, NIRV). Although this could be disruptive, it is also a good problem-solving skill. If Peter needs to know the answers, then asking someone else may be the solution.

Peter also needs clarity. During a meal with Jesus, Peter asks, "Why can't I follow you now?" (John 13:37, NIRV). He needs clarity concerning the details. For some things in life you just have to wait. Waiting can be hard for any of us, including Peter.

When all else fails, Peter's willingness to be honest remains. He might lie, but he is honest. Contradictory? Yes, but such is a day in the life of Peter.

PETER ROCKED HIS WORLD

Jesus claimed He would build His church upon the truth of Peter's confession: "You are the Christ, the Son of the living God" (Matthew 16:18). The name Peter in the New Testament language is related to "stone" or "rock." Jesus saw usefulness in Peter. Despite his impulsive drive, Jesus saw the potential to build upon this rock. Do you see that in your child? Several of the impulsive children and adolescents I have worked with displayed similar potential, and they knew it. Many times these kids know they have a calling on their lives. They know they were created for something more. Getting into trouble often becomes an easy excuse for many impulsive children and adolescents. It can be used as an escape or a tactic to avoid things or a way to help them get by. Even if your Peter knows the calling on his life, he will also need someone to believe in him, someone willing to water the seeds of growth like Jesus did. Jesus built into Peter's life. Peter grew from that and rocked the world around him.

CUTTING THINGS DOWN TO SIZE

Peter finds success in small numbers. Whenever possible, your Peter should work in small groups. It helps to build rapport, and it tends to make Peter more comfortable and more manageable as well. Remember, the disciple Peter was often found in a small group with only Jesus and John. Placing too many Peters in one group could also be setting up the group for failure. Too much of a good thing is definitely not a good thing with regard to impulsiveness.

WHENEVER POSSIBLE, YOUR PETER SHOULD WORK IN SMALL GROUPS.

Jesus trusted Peter. He often took Peter aside in small groups because He trusted him. On one occasion when Peter was in a small group with Jesus, Jesus' appearance changed right before their eyes (Mark 9:2). Jesus wasn't willing to share that with everyone, but Jesus trusted the small group. He trusted Peter.

Small group settings also open up the opportunity for your Peter to concentrate. Within these settings, your Peter can learn to ask appropriate questions privately. Peter practiced this with Jesus in Mark 13:3. Use small group settings to train your Peter in appropriateness. Model for him how to ask questions properly and privately when acceptable.

Jesus wanted to have Peter in small groups to teach him. Mark 5:37 (NIRV) says, "[Jesus] let only Peter, James, and John, the brother of James, follow him." Seek out ways to place your Peter in a small group atmosphere whenever possible, especially, when you want him to learn. Advocate for Peter, if necessary, because your Peter is most likely to find success in these small settings.

ANOTHER ONE BITES THE DUST

Sleeping problems are prevalent among ADHD (Attention Deficit Hyperactivity Disorder) kids. "About half of parents of children with ADHD report that their children have difficulty sleeping, feel tired on waking, or have nightmares or other sleep problems such as disordered breathing and restless leg syndrome."[13] In his article, *Treating ADHD with a Better Night's Sleep*, William Dodson, M. D. explained that ADHD is a round-the-clock disorder and does not go away because the child is suppose to be sleeping.[14] Some clinicians believe that sleep problems contribute to misdiagnosis among ADHD suffers.

Recent research has verified that chronic poor sleep results in daytime tiredness, difficulties with focused attention, low thresholds to express negative emotions (irritability and easy frustration), and difficulty modulating impulses and emotions (Seminars in Pediatric Neurology, Mar 1996). These are the same symptoms that can earn kids the diagnosis of ADHD. ADD is an important problem in its own right, but research in sleep laboratories has shown that some (and perhaps a great many) kids are mislabeled with ADD when the real problem is chronic, partial sleep deprivation.[15]

This is important to note because sleep-deprived children, especially boys, can be misdiagnosed for exhibiting similar characteristics to those with ADHD. If your child is not sleeping, *then start with sleep!*

Guess what we find regarding Impulsive Peter? He also had sleep issues.

> *[Jesus] returned to his disciples and found them sleeping. 'Simon,' he said to Peter, 'Are you asleep? Couldn't you keep watch for one hour? Watch and pray. Then you won't fall into sin when you are tempted. The spirit is willing. But the body is weak'* (Mark 14:37-38, NIRV).

Isn't that true of Peter? His spirit was willing, but he was weak. You can teach your Peter by modeling prayer the same way Jesus did.

PETERS NEED THEIR SLEEP.

A sleepy Peter was mentioned on more than one occasion. For example in Luke 9:32 we find, "Peter and his companions had been very sleepy" (NIRV). Peters need their sleep. Help your Peter find ways to get sleep. Adequate sleep is key for him to find success. How does your Peter do this? Start by creating quiet bedtime routines. Shut off the electronics (start early with Peter), take a warm bath, spend some time cuddling and reading, and shut off the lights early. Consistent bedtime routines are generally the most effective. If all else fails (and it might), seek professional assistance. You all deserve a good night's sleep.

If your Peter is afraid or bothered by something before bed, it is best to address it before he attempts to sleep. Confront any issues and pray together. Inviting Jesus to sleep in your child's room may also help. It is precious to hear our three-year-old welcome Jesus into his room with his own short prayer, "Jesus, please come sleep with me." This is truly the safest sleepover your child may ever experience.

When our oldest was a newborn, I longed for a nightly prayer that incorporated Scripture for him. I wanted something simple, something small, something I could easily remember. The prayer "Now I lay me down to sleep"[16] no longer worked for our family. The mention of death did not sit well with me as a new mom. There is nothing wrong with that prayer, but I wanted something more for my family, something backed by Scripture. As I prayed, this is what transpired. I have prayed this over our children every night since:

"Father, thank you for (child's name).
Please quiet him (or her) with your love.
Help him (or her) lie down and
sleep in peace with sweet sleep,
Lord, we pray.
Let your angels surround him (or her) and
Protect him (or her) both through the night and the day.
And your protection cover over him (or her)
like a blanket, we ask.
In Jesus' name we pray. Amen."

CHAPTER 5
THE FUTURE OF PETER
And what do you do with him?

What do you do with a Peter? *You love him.* A Peter, girl or boy, may grate your every nerve, or be anything but a vacation to raise. But what Peter needs most is your love, and to love him is your main calling. All children need such love. All changeling children, whether they are fearful, filled with anxiety, hyperactive, or depressed, require one main thing, love! Give Peter your love. May his heart be stamped with your love for him.

Simon Peter was a priority to Jesus, so much so that He even renamed Peter (Luke 6:14). Simon Peter was repeatedly singled out from the beginning. He was on the top of Jesus' list. Has your impulsive child ever been placed at the top of any lists? Singled out, perhaps? When the teacher is absent and leaving instructions for the substitute, does your Peter become a top priority? Does the instruction sheet she holds read something like this? "And the desk beside mine. The little boy with red hair. His name is Peter. Keep a close eye on him."

> **WHAT PETER NEEDS MOST IS YOUR LOVE, AND TO LOVE HIM IS YOUR MAIN CALLING.**

Jesus singled Peter out. But it was not to criticize him for his behavior. It was always to mature Peter. He was chosen by Jesus and pulled out of the group. Remember that if your Peter appears on the top of many lists, or if you are placing him at the top of the list for any of the wrong reasons. Peter was important to Jesus. Peter was at the top of Jesus' list not because He couldn't handle Peter. It was because Jesus wanted to see Peter grow. Your Peter is important whether he ever makes the list or not. Some Peters will not make any lists, while others will never make it off the wrong lists. Pray through those lists then turn your focus toward Peter. What matters is that your Peter is included and is valuable to Jesus. Your Peter can make Jesus' list (Revelation 3:5). Your Peter qualifies for the list that matters, and it's all about maturing him.

OBEDIENCE MATTERS

Luke 5:1-11

Peter's lessons in obedience came as his walk with Jesus matured. Obedience is important. It is fundamental to parents and to Christians. Teach your children the importance of obeying. Pray and ask the Lord to bless your children with obedient hearts.

Peter acted in obedience, while also exhibiting incredible amounts of faith at one of the Lord's challenges (Luke 5:1-11). Jesus wanted Peter to return to the sea after fishing the entire night without a single catch. Can you imagine that as a fisherman? You are a professional and have spent all night working your tail off. Only to have nothing to show for it. You did not earn a dime from all that work and tireless energy. You pull into shore, start cleaning things up, and then some preacher climbs into your boat. After the initial shock wears off, you find you are intrigued by Him. You allow Him to stay. You listen as you work, then His lesson begins to stir within you.

You stop thinking of casting Him out so you can return home, and find yourself in tune with what He is saying. The fact is you are being reeled into His stories. You know there is something real, something more with Jesus. When His story finally ends and the people are gone, Jesus instructs you to go back out into the sea. Jesus says, "Put out into the deep and let down your nets for a catch.' And Simon Peter answered, 'Master, we toiled all night and took nothing! But at your word I will let down the nets'" (Luke 5:4-5). After working all night long, what did they have to show for it? NOTHING! And Jesus still asked Peter to do it all over again. Everything was cleaned up. Everything was put away, and still Jesus wanted Peter to obey. Listen to Jesus, especially when you have nothing. He wants obedience (1 Samuel 15:22, NIV). He wanted Peter to obey.

Peter's obedience was rewarded with a boatload of fish. Luke 5:6 says, "And when they had done this, they enclosed a large number of fish, and their nets were breaking." Peter's ship finally came in. This is a great reminder of endurance. *Your Peter is to never give up!* Have him keep trying. You never know when his ship is about to overflow. Teach him the importance of remaining obedient. Pray about this for him. Then do not give up hope for your Peter. In essence Jesus said,

"Keep on trying, Peter. Do not give up. Listen and obey me. The fish are out there, try again."

Astonished by the wonder of his catch, Peter falls at the feet of Jesus. Then he says, "Depart from me, for I am a sinful man, O Lord" (Luke 5:8). Peter knew his place. He recognized who he was in light of a holy God. He had no trouble distinguishing between the two. As careless as Peter could be, he actually was quite humble. These fishermen just received the largest haul of their lives, and they left it all at the shore for Jesus (Luke 5:11). Could you or I do that? Could your Peter do that?

Peter and the others left their nets behind to follow Jesus. Is your child free from any nets? Sometimes nets can act as a trap. "The arrogant have hidden a trap for me, and with cords they have spread a net; beside the way they have set snares for me" (Psalm 140:5). For Peter to live safely, ask God to remove all hidden traps and nets (Psalm 141:10; Psalm 142:3).

PREPARING PETER
John 18:15-16; John 13:6-10; Luke 22:8-13
Continuing Peter's story, Jesus was later taken into the high priest's courtyard. The disciple John was allowed in, while Peter remained outside. He could not go into the inner circle (John 18:15-16, NIRV). Peter stood around waiting as others passed him. He did not have inside connections with anyone except Jesus. Are there times when your Peter is standing around, waiting for his turn? Is your Peter left outside the inner circle as

peers, siblings, or even his enemies pass him by? Do they get in before your Peter? Remember, Peter's time eventually came even if the others had already passed him (John 18:16, NIRV).

Help your Peter feel successful by highlighting his positive behaviors. Point out to him specific times and places when impulsiveness is good, including emergency situations. It's good to be the first to respond in many cases. This is impulsive Peter, and impulsiveness is not always a bad thing. Highlight the qualities for him.

Train your Peter to know limits. Train him to know when enough is enough. While counseling some impulsive adolescents, I have used the children's book, *If You Give a Mouse a Cookie.*[17] At the conclusion of the story, we would recap and discuss similarities the young person shared with the never-satisfied-mouse. We processed limits and discussed behaviors that exemplified satisfaction. This is really developing the fruit of self-control. You may also need to go situation by situation and give specifics to your Peter. Think about the Last Supper when Jesus washed the disciples' feet (John 13:6-10). Peter needed specifics. At first, he had a problem with Jesus washing his feet. After Jesus' explanation, Peter suddenly felt the need for a complete bath, but Jesus lovingly told him, "No, what I'm doing is enough." Identify where your Peter struggles. When is enough, enough? Be specific in the situation. What is tolerable and acceptable behavior, and what is not? Crazy as it may sound, your Peter really may not know.

TRAIN YOUR PETER TO KNOW LIMITS.

Peter needed Jesus to establish limits for him. He essentially did this when He said, "This is enough" (John 13:6-10, NIRV). Are you setting up limits for your child? Limits will look different from household to household, but Peters need limits. Set healthy limits for him to follow. The Ten Commandments are in place because we all need some established rules. Research repeatedly points to the fact that children are more likely to thrive in a consistent, structured environment. Does your Peter have that? Do not shame yourself if not, but don't stop there either. Ask God to help you, and then start to establish a few simple limits.

To prepare for Passover, Peter was given a job to do along with John in Luke 22:8. Jesus gave Peter certain tasks to accomplish that He knew Peter could complete successfully. "[Peter and John] found things just as Jesus had told them. So they prepared the Passover meal" (Luke 22:13, NIRV). The job was complete. Give your Peter jobs to do, but make sure he can complete those tasks with success.

Collaborate with Peter's teachers, counselors, and other trusted individuals on acceptable behaviors for Peter in various scenarios. Then have Peter practice these acceptable behaviors in music class, on the bus, visiting his grandparents in the retirement home, or at a play date at the park. Start practicing in the places where Peter is likely to fall apart. Practice! Your Peter may never get things perfect, but *practice will help.*

BECOMING STRONG

Matthew 26:69-75; John 21:15-19

To look at Peter's future, you must consider that his past included denying Jesus. Does your Peter deny anything in the past? What is your solution for denial? Three times Peter denied knowing Jesus. Likewise, Jesus addressed each breach of loyalty by fully restoring Peter (John 21:15-19). Does your Peter need to be restored? Does your relationship with him need any restoration? You may need to address each circumstance for your Peter to receive complete healing. Quiet yourself and listen to God's voice. While you are asking, also ask God to reveal any times your Peter has been denied.

Your Peter will fail. Not once or twice, but three times, and probably many more. The disciple Peter did fail the Lord (Matthew 26:69-75). Publicly and privately Peter failed, but he always rebounded. Peter never stopped. He was resilient. How do you respond to your Peter's failures? Jesus took the positive route and spoke into Peter's life, "When you have turned back, help your brothers to be strong" (Luke 22:32, NIRV). Jesus knew Peter would fail Him, but He encouraged Peter's return. Jesus' future focus was on forgiveness, the very forgiveness He knew Peter would need.

At the time when Peter denied knowing Jesus, he had little backbone. Peter was just a mere follower until a later time when he was literally made strong. It was almost as if this failure, this complete disregard for Jesus, pushed him farther ahead in the end. It made his belief stronger. He talked about Christ and stood up for Him everywhere once he stopped wasting time in the crowd. Your Peter might be a follower for a season. But like Peter, a dominant leader may reside deep within. This is not meant to encourage following the crowd, but it is meant to offer hope. Remember who is in control. Pray that your Peter will triumph like the disciple Peter did. Think of all the places Peter had to come from in order to get to this point. Do not take the backseat approach in parenting your Peter. Get actively involved. But keep in mind that *Peter's walk is about the journey*, not just a few incidents along the way.

Your Peter will make many mistakes. Some will be large and some small. But he will fail. He will fail you, he will fail teachers, and he will ultimately fail God. But be thankful for redemption because we all fail (Romans 3:23). But at the same time, do not set your Peter up for failure. Do not establish beforehand that he will fail every time and cannot succeed. That is different from what I am suggesting. The likelihood is that Peter will fail. But make it permissible because he is human and not because he himself is a failure. He will fail, so give him permission to do so and to try again. Success can be built upon failure, thus becoming a way for Peter to win!

YOUR PETER WILL FAIL.

Satan wanted to sift Peter and the disciples (Luke 22:31-32). But Jesus interceded, and prayed that Peter's faith would not fail. Jesus' prayer had nothing to do with Peter's failures. Jesus was more concerned that Peter's faith would not fail. *Faith was the driving force in Peter.* Jesus probably hated watching Peter fail, but he knew that it was Peter's faith that was critical. Faith is the pick-me-up after failing, and it's also faith that sustains us when our circumstances seem overwhelming. When everything within us wants to give up, faith pulls us through. Jesus prayed that Peter's faith or his pick-me-up would not fail.

With the return of Head Coach Chuck Pagano to the Indianapolis Colts after his hospitalization in 2012, the club and fan base were inspired from his fight against leukemia. The term ChuckStrong was created from that strong fight as he encouraged folks everywhere. Likewise, with the help of Jesus' intercession, the disciple Peter also came back strong. In his return, he became PeterStrong. Peter's return to Jesus helped others find strength. Prayerfully ask God for unfailing faith for your Peter. Pray that your Peter's faith will not fail, even though he might. Pray even when problems surround your Peter. Pray that his faith will not fail him. With unfailing faith, your Peter will have the ability to turn back and bring others with him. But first, intercede for your Peter as Jesus did.

Satan wanted the disciples, including Peter, to believe they were worthless. Perhaps Satan saw what others missed. Maybe he saw the potential in Peter, and knew Peter would be a great threat to him. He asked specifically for him. Do not lose hope when your Peter faces trials of many kinds (Psalm 34:19, NIRV; James 1:2, NIV). Know that the enemy sees the threat within your Peter. *Peter was a threat.* Do not lose hope. Dig in and dig deep. Do not let faith fail you or your Peter. Being threatened is actually a compliment to your Peter's capability. Consequences came rapidly after Peter's denial, and his remorse was great. "Peter remembered… And he went out and wept bitterly" (Matthew 26:75). Peter had regrets. He had remorse because he loved Jesus. Peter's regrets were written all over his face, and he felt the immediate results of his sin. As Peter's parents, do not delay administering consequences for your Peter's misbehaviors. Consequences may be hard for your Peter, but situations are most relevant to him within an immediate timeframe.

Galatians 1:10 (NIV) says, "Am I now trying to win the approval of human beings, or of God? Or am I trying to please people? If I were still trying to please people, I would not be a servant of Christ." Peter may have responded out of fear, when he denied knowing Jesus. But this verse reminds us not to be motivated by fear or by pleasing others. At this point Peter was acting as a follower, just trying to fit in. He may have been saying, "I want to be close enough to Jesus to see what is going on. I care about Him. But I have to deny the truth because I am afraid of these people and what they might think." Peter wanted to be in close proximity. In his heart, he probably wanted to do the right thing. But at this point, he was not strong enough. He still worried about what others thought and feared the consequences of following his Lord. When confronted with the truth, he denied it. Give your young Peter grace as he learns, but continually challenge him to grow. One day when Peter's passion and persistence collide, he will become the leader God intended for him to be.

MATURITY, AHOY!

Luke 10:11-12; Mark 16:6-7; John 20:1-10; John 21:1-19

At times, Peter's impulsiveness put him ahead of the pack, and that created confusion for him. "Peter ... ran to the tomb ... saw the strips ... and went away, wondering what had happened" (Luke 24:12, NIRV). Eventually with the help of others, Peter would put the pieces together and figure out what occurred. Because of impulsiveness, your Peter could end up in uncertain circumstances. But if he does get ahead of the crowd, remind him that those around him also have abilities to also help him.

Check this out. After the death of Jesus an angel of the Lord appeared to Mary Magdalene. The angel said, "Go! Tell his disciples and *Peter* (emphasis mine), 'He is going ahead of you...'" (Mark 16:6, NIRV). Jesus had Peter's number, and He knew him by name. (Isaiah 43:1). He wanted Peter to know he was still included. Peter was still one of His. God had the angel call the disciples *and Peter.* Notice God called all of the disciples, but Peter was the only one specifically named. I believe this small act also planted hope within Peter. Jesus sent the message ahead. He let Peter know ahead of time that he was still included. What a beautiful reconciliation piece for Peter who probably doubted his relationship with Christ at this point. This inclusive reminder might be just what your Peter needs after a fall. Likewise, God also cares about your Peter, and He knows him by name.

Simon Peter went back to fishing after the death of Jesus (John 21:3). Peter did not know what to do when the plans failed. When your plans fail, your Peter will most likely revert back to his old patterns and behaviors. He will likely slip back into the old ways because they are familiar to him. What appeared to work for him in the past in all likelihood will be what he does once again.

Peter needed to be busy doing something. He had nothing to do now without Jesus. He needed direction. Without it, he returned to fishing. Peter knew he was able to do that. It was at least something to do. He needed to fish. Your Peter will need something to do. As you develop your plans for him, continue to reestablish what is already working and keep trying to progress forward.

WHEN YOUR PLANS FAIL, YOUR PETER WILL MOST LIKELY REVERT BACK TO HIS OLD PATTERNS AND BEHAVIORS.

Does your Peter ever set things down like his coat, his hat, his wallet, or his lunch money and then forget about it? In typical Peter-like-fashion, biblical Peter took off his coat and laid it down (John 21:7, NIRV). Anything ever come up missing with your Peter? Peter's things may fill most of the Lost and Found areas at school. But notice something has changed in the disciple Peter as the story continues. This time before Peter ran, he picked up his coat and put it back on (John 21:7). He had not forgotten where it was. This was a sign of Peter maturing. When the disciples spotted Jesus on the shore, it was Peter's natural response to jump right in. He did not wait for the boat to be docked. Frankly, he did not have time. He did not care about the water or getting wet. His thoughts were strictly focused upon Jesus. Why should Peter wait when he could get there faster? This is a part of Peter I love and feel we should desperately desire. *Peter let nothing, absolutely nothing, hold him back.* This is one instance where Peter's impulsiveness was great! Keep in mind, not all impulsiveness is bad. This is one of those instances. Look for ways to positively enhance your Peter's impulsiveness. Discover the good in his character. Peter desperately needs to know how to channel and handle the gift of impulsiveness. Then it will become a gift.

Peter is no longer immature. Following Peter's swim, he obeyed Jesus and went aboard the boat to retrieve breakfast (John 21:11). Peter completed the tasks Jesus gave to him. Remember, it is important to give your Peter tasks to do. He will respond. Collaborate with his teachers to create jobs for Peter. Break up the most difficult parts of his day by giving him a positive task to complete. If the afternoon is a challenging period, try to incorporate work alternatives during that part of his day. Working with your Peter's internal schedule is not always possible, but it will likely yield the greatest rewards. Investing time reaps great rewards.

As we continue the story, Peter and Jesus are on the beach together. What do you do at the beach? Do you sunbathe, walk, build a sandcastle, or play a game of catch? This was not a time for vacation for Jesus. He got right to work and faced Peter's denials three separate times (John 21:15-19).

The entire time Jesus was asking Peter questions, He was also disciplining Peter. Jesus is a master at utilizing tough love, and this is no exception. However, he was also reinstating Peter at the same time. Jesus gave Peter specific instructions to follow. But it took three times! Three times to be corrected and three times to be reinstated. "Peter felt bad because Jesus asked him the third time" (John 21:17, NIRV). Most Peters are tenderhearted like our biblical friend, Peter. It will hurt when

CONFRONTATION IS NEVER EASY.

you repeatedly question his loyalty. It would hurt any of us to stand before the Lord and have our love for him questioned. But Jesus continued out of love. Confrontation is never easy, but *sometimes confrontation is the only way to love* (Ephesians 4:15, NIV).

If you need constructive assignments for your Peter, try these. As Jesus corrected Peter, He said, "Feed my lambs" (John 21:15). Generally, most Peters work well with children (or lambs). In corporate settings, allow your Peter to serve little lambs. Lambs are the young or the weaker ones within the flock. Try having your Peter serve as an assistant in Sunday school, as a peer mentor within a supervised setting at school, or as the bat boy for the little league team. The list is endless, but assignments are needed and must be purposeful. Peter needed direction. He also needed something to do.

Utilizing service as a part of your Peter's discipline has multiple benefits. First, these assignments give him something to do. Peter needs something to occupy his time. It also provides your Peter with positive regard for service in his community. Remember, society often uses restitution as a positive form of punishment. It is often in the form of community service. In addition, it also offers a social venue for Peter and those he serves. Serving possibilities should incorporate your Peter's unique abilities. For some, you may want to explore the possibilities of caring for animals at home or as a volunteer at the local animal shelter.

In the second reinstatement Jesus said, "Take care of my sheep" (John 21:16, NIRV). Give your Peter opportunities to care for others. Nursing homes depend upon volunteers, and your Peter may be just what they are looking for. Let your Peter help take out the trash, pull weeds in your flower beds, or shovel your elderly neighbor's driveway. Give your Peter tangible ways to participate and take care of people.
In Jesus' final response to Peter's denial, He again repeated, "Feed my sheep" (John 21:17, NIRV). What does that mean? Peter was to teach others about God by feeding them. Teaching a hungry soul about God can be satisfying both to the giver and the receiver. Feeding God's sheep was an assignment that would benefit both worlds. Peter told others about Jesus. He was bright, bold, and courageous. Offer your Peter safe venues to express light. Maybe your Peter could influence others through playing music at the retirement home, giving a Bible to someone, performing in an Easter production, organizing a fundraiser for missions, or by being a bell ringer for charity at Christmas.

It has been said that we learn the most when we teach. Use

your Peter's knowledge to apply this truth. Whatever it may be that your Peter knows best, help him use it to influence others. All Peters remain individuals and will have different needs, desires, and talents. What works for one Peter may not work with another. This may be tested by trial and error. However, you need to find what works for your Peter. What are his gifts and talents? What is he good at, and how can he use it?

What were the suggestions for your Peter's constructive rehabilitation? Encourage him to offer help to little ones, physically care for others, and share his knowledge with them. Try these constructive venues and help him see them through. Your follow-through will make all the difference in the world.

In the meantime, do not let your Peter get hung up on what others are doing. Biblical Peter had a tendency to turn around and lose focus. Once he was turned around, Peter started concentrating on what others were receiving, what he was missing

REMIND HIM TO MIND HIS OWN BUSINESS AND MOVE FORWARD.

out on, and whether it was fair. Jesus tells Peter, however, "Don't worry about the other guy. Worry about yourself" (John 21:20-22, NIRV). Your Peter may also lose focus if he starts concentrating on what others are doing and what he is missing out on. Remind him to mind his own business and move forward (1 Thessalonians 4:11, NIRV).

As we close this chapter on Peter, remember he is never too old to play. Spend time together playing with your Peter. Whether it is his favorite sport or a game of cards, play with your Peter. The memories you create will be enjoyed for a lifetime.

That's not all! Simon Peter from the Gospels transforms in the book of Acts into a man with incredible force, boldness, and empowered from the Holy Spirit. Now he was focused, ready, grown-up, and mature. Peter was a man of actions both big and small. Over time and as a result of the death of Jesus, Peter had matured to become a strong man. He was now considered a leader. When he told the other disciples he was going somewhere, they followed.

Many shudder to think how similar they are to Simon Peter's negative traits, and yet we should long to possess the positives that characterized the mature Peter. Keep in mind as you parent, as you counsel, and as you love, *it was Peter who took a chance to believe when no one else believed* (Luke 24:10-12).

THE GAME PLAN FOR IMPULSIVE PETER

1. Emphasize Positives
2. Train Peter to Think Biblical Thoughts Concerning Himself
3. Monitor Your Voice Tone
4. Give Peter Frequent Breaks
5. Spend Time Together Following Discipline
6. Help Peter Identify the Source of Rushing Sensations
7. Give Peter Reminders Including Thoughtful Glances and Cues
8. Provide Small Group Settings that Model Appropriate Behaviors
9. Train Peter to Recognize and Know Limits
10. Supply Peter with Details that Will Impact His Day
11. Identify Areas of Struggle for Your Peter
12. Practice Useful Behaviors in Place of Careless Impulsiveness
13. Provide Your Peter with Tasks that Build Success
14. Develop Non-harmful Alternatives to Aggression
15. Know the Difference Between Peter's Innocent Acts and Deliberate Disobedience
16. Be Actively Involved
17. Provide Your Peter with Situations Where Impulsiveness is Good
18. Provide Constructive Forms of Rehabilitation that Act as Assignments
19. Address Lying Through Repetitious Reinstating
20. Play Together

CHAPTER 6
PRAYER FOR YOUR CHILD

This is where the work begins. Parents of Peters may not want to hear that there is more work to do. *But there is!* You have been given some tools to assist your child, but true spiritual change happens when we get on our knees. Assume a comfortable position because now is the time to work.

> *Lord, I come believing that (child's name) can be changed. I repent of any damaging thoughts that hold (child's name) back. Please heal any brokenness I have created out of haste or frustration. Please forgive any wounds that exist from my negligence or the negligence of others. I repent and am sorry. Please forgive me. "Create in me a pure heart, O God, and renew a steadfast spirit within me," according to Psalm 51:10 (NIV). Lord, I cannot do this alone. Parenting my Peter is more than I can handle some days. I do not have enough inside of me to help him. Please recreate me, and fill me full with everything I need to help transform my Simon into a Peter.*
>
> *I pray that (child's name) will be helpful and not hurtful to himself or to others. Overflow his heart with the fruit of Your Spirit.[1] Lord, I lift up (child's name) to You. May Your loving arms surround (child's name). Please restore, confirm, strengthen, and establish (child's name).[2]*

1. Galatians 5:22-23, 2. 1 Peter 5:10

Please heal (child's name) of any curses he has cast upon himself, and please free him from the curses of others. In Christ (child's name) is a new creation,[3] and he is complete. I pray newness, peace, and freedom into the life of this child. (Child's name) desperately needs this, Lord. I ask that You transform (child's name) by renewing his mind.[4] Thank you for giving (child's name) the mind of Christ.[5] Please think Your thoughts through him. I ask that no weapon formed against (child's name) will prosper.[6] Rescue (child's name) from every evil attack of the enemy,[7] and please give him the protection of Your kingdom.[8] Please remove any hidden traps for (child's name).[9] Make (child's name) new and free.[10] The old is now gone from (child's name).[11]

I ask that my Peter's impulsive speech be transformed into quiet listening. Help (child's name) to be "quick to hear, slow to speak, slow to anger." [12] Produce the righteousness that You require within him, Lord.

Help me to be straight forward and to the point with my Peter. Please create room for us to love one another. Lord, please bless me with creative and useful ideas to help (child's name). Help me to utilize his skills as part of the discipline in his life. Please keep me from belittling or putting down my child, and becoming easily frustrated with him. Please also keep (child's name) from feeling put down elsewhere. Let our home and our family become a safe place where (child's name) is built up and

3. 2 Corinthians 5:17, 4. Romans 12:2, 5. 1 Corinthians 2:16,
6. Isaiah 54:17, 7. 2 Timothy 4:18, 8. Psalm 141:10, 9. Psalm 142:3,
10. John 8:36, 11. 2 Corinthians 5:17, 12. James 1:19

*restored. Make us like a sanctuary from the storm for this child.
Show me (child's name)'s gifts. Help us create useful plans for
(child's name). Allow the plans to replenish and mature (child's
name) when mistakes happen. Help (child's name) forgive and
receive forgiveness for his sins.*

*As parents, we need to do what is necessary for (child's name) to
be successful, but we need Your help, Lord. Please show us what
to do. Help us create useful tasks for (child's name) to build
success upon. Show me how Jesus did this for His disciple Peter.
Help me establish healthy limits. Please give us wisdom.[13] Help
me to train my (child's name) in the tangible ways that You
love him. Teach me how to train him, and give him a heart
built to endure. I ask, Father God, that (child's name)'s faith
will never fail him as Jesus prayed for His Peter.[14] May (child's
name) know and believe the love that You have for him.[15]*

*God, You know my child's need for sleep. Please grant restful,
peaceful sleep for (child's name) because of Your love.[16] I declare
Your love over (child's name). Thank You that You do love him,
Lord.[17] May (child's name) know that You are for him and not
against him.[18]*

*Guide me in giving (child's name) firm instruction. Grant
me the energy to repair mistakes and then carry on with Your
plans for us. Change my heart not to focus upon the mistakes
as setbacks to Your plan. Train me, like Jesus, to know the*

13. James 1:5, 14. Luke 22:32, 15. 1 John 4:16,
16. Psalm 127:2, 17. 1 John 4:7-10, 18. Romans 8:31

difference between acts of disobedience and the innocent acts my Peter creates. Help me do more than just hang on, Lord. Equip me with strength for every battle.[19] I no longer want to settle for mediocrity. Help me to identify my child's positives and encourage him to be all that You created him to be. Help me to spiritually equip (child's name). Please pave the path for us to follow, and harbor us from attacks. I need Your help, Lord. Thank You that every battle belongs to You.[20] I pray that (child's name) will triumph like biblical Peter did.

Lord, please give me wisdom[21] and an open heart to see when (child's name) truly repents. Also help me to forgive just as You have forgiven me.[22] Please strengthen (child's name), and help him to be more concerned about what You think than what others think.[23] Lord, please always be gracious to (child's name), and show him mercy.[24] Even though biblical Peter denied You, You restored him each time. Lord, please respond in a similar way to (child's name). Please gently restore him when he fails.

Help me to wait upon You and not to rush Your hand.[25] Please show me Your plan for (child's name). Help (child's name) to mature into the man You are creating him to be. Make (child's name) a man of action for Your kingdom with incredible force, boldness, zest for life, and Holy Spirit-directed movements all the days of his life.

---

19. Psalm 18:39, 20. 2 Chronicles 20:15, 21. James 1:5, 22. Colossians 3:13, 23. Galatians 1:10; 1 Thessalonians 2:4, 24. Isaiah 30:18, 25. Psalm 33:20

Lord, I repent and ask for forgiveness if there is anything standing in the way of my believing the best for my Peter's life. Help me to look beyond the past. I ask and believe all these things for (child's name) in Jesus' name, and repent of any doubts I may have concerning Your best for my Peter. Thank you, Lord, for all You created (child's name) to be.
In Jesus' name, Amen.

CHAPTER 7
THE LOVING HEART

You have made it this far! Congratulations! May your heart be encouraged because working with kids can be a challenge. Difficulties may arise as you grapple to understand and love them in appropriate ways. Most assuredly obstacles will arise. Overcoming obstacles can be a tiring feat especially as the battle rages. But, you are doing it. You are trying. Keep working. *Don't give up!* If you do, who will fight for this child? Who will help him? Who will lead him? Think of the possibilities. *This child needs you!*

"Children are a gift from the Lord," and they need to be valued (Psalm 127:3, NLT). One of the greatest gifts I have found is learning to value life, both mine and the lives of others. While still in the learning process, the more I dive into this knowledge the more abundant life I find. Life is a gift. It is worth valuing, whether it's mine or someone else's. Our lives have significance. The world is a better place just because we exist. Nothing else in the world retains such significance. All other assets fall short of placing value on another's life.

When I value life, I do things differently. My every day, mundane tasks take on purpose as I respond to my husband or disciple my children (1 Corinthians 9:26, NLT). Valuing their lives transforms me. I long to be a great mom without yelling at my kiddos. Apart from valuing who God created them to be, I fall short, and this becomes nothing more than a lofty ambition. Acknowledging the value of another's life adds greater significance to my intentions, resulting in purposeful interactions. Like them or not, value them or not, the folks around me do have significance. *Life matters.*

GOD CREATED YOUR CHILD, AND HE MATTERS.

How do you acknowledge that there is purpose to life? By placing value on who your child is and for whom he was created. God created your child, and he matters. Hopefully, he matters to you. But heaven knows his value is far beyond your capability to love.

Which brings us to investing in the life of your child. It is risky to be involved in anyone's life. You are taking a chance with regard to *this child*, but *you are also here for a reason*. You are being given the opportunity to be a real-life hero! You can be used in the life of *this child*, but you cannot give up! Walk in truth and seek God's ways. At times, you may need to fight on behalf of *this child*, all the while remembering who the enemy is. The fight is not against *this child* or any other person for that matter. Know your enemy (Ephesians 6:12). When you go to battle for *this child*, cast your cares upon God because He cares for you. As you do, He will grant you peace that surpasses your ability to understand (1 Peter 5:7; Philippians 4:7). Trust God with the hopes and fears you have regarding *this child*.

APPLYING GOD'S PROMISES

Let your prayer for *this child* be when he "passes through the waters, that God will be with him; and through the rivers, that they shall not overwhelm him; when he walks through the fire, he shall not be burned, and the flames shall not consume him" (Isaiah 43:2, author's paraphrase). God's promise is that He will never leave your child despite how the circumstances appear.

This really is a battle. There is a war going on outside your front door. A thief wants your child (John 10:10). The enemy will use anything. Low self-worth, fear, anxiety, impulsiveness, and depression can all be used against your child when you least expect them. Do not kid yourself, Satan's only purpose is to devour your child (1 Peter 5:8). As Christ-followers, we know the ultimate war has *already been won* (Revelation 17:14). But as the days grow increasingly darker leading up to that final war, *we must prepare our children to stand* (Ephesians 6:10-18). That's where you and I come in.

NEVER STOP!

Never stop loving *this child*. Never stop believing in this child. Never stop caring for *this child*. Never stop praying for *this child*. Prayer works (James 5:16). Create a network of trusted individuals to pray on behalf of your child. Ask them to pray regularly, and update them as needs arise. Your unceasing prayers will foster love, belief, and care in the life of *this child*. Never stop trusting in God. When you trust in something other than God, you will collapse and fall. But those that trust in God will rise (Psalm 20:7-8). Prayer is also a continual act of trust. It's trusting God to take care of your requests and desires. In essence, when you pray you are actually saying, "God, I trust you with this." Prayerfully trust God with *this child*.

Let everything you do for *this child* be unto the Lord (Colossians 3:17). As you do, allow Psalm 103, Zephaniah 3:17, and Ephesians 3:18-19 to become the anthems of your heart. "Be strong in the Lord and in the power of His might" (Ephesians 6:10). May you one day hear, "Well done," and receive the greatest joy in knowing this child walks in truth because you cared (Matthew 25:21; 3 John 1:4). *Stamp this on your child's heart.*

PRAYER FOR YOU AND YOUR CHILD

Lord, You have chosen me to do what is right. Please take hold of my hand, and keep me safe. Help me to value the life of this child, and cause me to see (child's name) as the gift you intended him to be.[1] Use me in the life of (child's name). Make me a light to (child's name). Open his eyes, set him free, and release him from any darkness. Lord, in order to do this I must become pure. I repent of my sins and ask forgiveness. Help me to forgive because I have been forgiven. I'm offering every care and concern that I have to You. I repent of any self-righteous acts I have committed, and I draw near to You. I need Your fresh understanding, wisdom, and love.

You are the Lord! That is Your name! You will not let another god share Your glory or Your praise. What You say goes! Lord, please announce new things to (child's name) in Jesus' name.

1. *Psalm 127:3*

*The old has gone, and the new has come.[2] I am sent to turn
(child's name) from darkness to light and from the power of
Satan to God, that (child's name) may receive forgiveness of sins
and a place among those who are sanctified by faith in You.[3]
God, You so loved this world that You gave Jesus. Your Word says
that whoever believes in Him will not perish, but have eternal
life.[4] I ask that (child's name) would believe in Jesus. May
(child's name) not perish but have eternal life. Lord, please be
tender, kind, gracious, slow to anger, and full of love concerning
(child's name). Show (child's name) that You will not punish
him as his sins deserve, and You will not repay him for the evil
he has done. Help (child's name) to respect You. Let Your love for
(child's name) rise as high as the heavens. Remove any lawless
acts from (child's name). Please be a tender, kind Father to
(child's name).[5] Lord God, You call (child's name) by his name.
Redeem (child's name), and help him not to be afraid.[6]*

*Lord, You care about (child's name). I ask because of Your
care for him. Please bind up his wounds and heal his broken
heart in Jesus' name.[7] Father God, You are with (child's name).
You are mighty enough to save (child's name). You take great
delight in (child's name). I ask that the quietness of Your love
calms (child's name) down. Lord, please sing over (name) with
joy as you did over Israel.[8] Lord, please forgive all his sins and
heal him.[9] Make me useful to remove obstacles out of (child's
name) way.[10] Lord, please be (child's name)'s shepherd; gather
him into Your arms; carry him close to Your heart, and then
gently lead us.[11]*

2. 2 Corinthians 5:17, 3. Acts 26:18, 4. John 3:16, 5. Psalm 103:8-13, NIRV
6. Matthew 10:31; John 14:27 NIRV, 7. Psalm 147:3, 8. Zephaniah 3:17, NIRV
9. Psalm 103:3, 10. Isaiah 57:14, 11. Isaiah 40:11

You are the everlasting God. You are not faint, and You do not grow weary. Your understanding is unsearchable.[12] Please give us strength when we are tired and power in exchange for our weakness. Even when (child's name) becomes tired and worn out or falls, increase our strength. Lord, help me to trust You! May we fly on wings like eagles. May we run and not be tired. May we walk and not grow weak.[13] Please give us peace to surpass all understanding to guard our hearts and minds in Christ Jesus.[14] Put a hedge of protection around us.[15] May Your faithful love be all around us because we trust You.[16]

Lord, please strengthen (child's name) with the power of Your Holy Spirit in his inner being, so that You may dwell in his heart through faith.[17] Lord, I ask for (child's name)'s love to have deep roots and a strong foundation. Grant (child's name) power with all Your people to understand Your love toward him. May (child's name) know how wide and long and high and deep Your love is.[18] May (child's name) know Your love even though it cannot be completely known. Please fill (child's name) with everything You have for him.[19] (Child's name) is from You. (Child's name) has overcome because You are in (child's name), and You are greater than he who is in the world.[20]

Please keep me from doubt and cause me to believe. Help me to not grow weary in doing good.[21] Lord, I am Your servant. You have chosen me to be involved in (child's name)'s life,

12. *Isaiah 40:28,* 3. *Isaiah 40:29-31, NIRV,* 14. *Philippians 4:7,* 15. *Job 1:10*
16. *Psalm 32:10, NIRV,* 17. *Ephesians 3:16-17,* 18. *Ephesians 3:18,*
19. *Ephesians 3:17-19, NIRV,* 20. *1 John 4:4, NKJV,* 21. *Galatians 6:9*

and You have not cast me off. Help me to not be afraid. You are with me. Please strengthen me, and help me. Uphold me with Your mighty right hand.[22] Father God, You "said to me, My grace (My favor, loving-kindness and mercy) is enough for you [sufficient against any danger and enables you to bear the trouble manfully]; for My strength and power are made perfect (fulfilled and completed) and show themselves most effective in [your] weakness," according to 2 Corinthians 12:9 (AMP). "Therefore, I will all the more gladly glory in my weaknesses and infirmities, that the strength and power of Christ (the Messiah) may rest (yes, may pitch a tent over and dwell) upon me" (2 Corinthians 12:9, AMP).

God, You alone are able! You are able to do far more than I could ask or imagine on behalf of (child's name). According to Your great power at work within us, please do that for (child's name).[23] Lord, help me understand how to use Your Word with power. May You heal and do powerful works and special things within (child's name).[24] Help us know the love that You have for us, and may we trust that love.[25] In Jesus' name, Amen.

22. *Isaiah 41:10,* 23. *Ephesians 3:20,* 24. *Acts 4:29-30, NLV,* 25. *1 John 4:16, NLT*

 # ACKNOWLEDGMENTS

Chad – How can I ever thank you! You let me try and help me perfect my gifts. Thank you! You are forever mine, and I am yours. I love you!

Jackson, Jeremiah, & Cole – I am forever grateful that I am your mom. I love each one of you with a crazy love! You're belief in me ignites my soul! Thank you, boys!

Mom & Dad – You have always believed in me! Your belief was so strong that I also began to believe. Thank you! I love you!

Corky – My mother-in-law who is also one of my cheerleaders! Thank you! Your love means a great deal to me!

Suzann – I'm grateful for your friendship and prayers. You have prayed for our boys before they were even born and over these books when they were simply a thought. I will always treasure you, my friend. Thank you for your constant love and support of my projects, my family, and for me. You are part of my spiritual family... *forever!* I love you, dear friend!

To all my praying friends and family – There are too many of you to mention, and I am completely humbled and grateful for each of you! I feel so honored to have you in my life! I am constantly reassured knowing that you are praying. Thank you for the many ways you have loved me and touched my life.

Thank you for playing a special part in this journey. I have some of the greatest friends of my life. I feel so blessed by each of you. I love you, and thank you!

Jodi – You were a champion of prayer for me with this project. I knew you were praying on the days I needed it most. Your prayers and encouraging words helped birth this book. Thank you, my friend! You are precious to me, and I love you!

Haley – You were exactly what an intern should be. You were ready to work, enthusiastic about any opportunity, and good at keeping me accountable so that I would complete this project. You were great to work with! Thank you! You are a gift and have a gift! God's blessings!

Jesse – My editing partner who helped me solidify my thoughts while keeping matters biblically sound. Thank you for all your help! You were great to work with!

Lord – Thank You for all You do for me! May You be glorified!

END NOTES

1. Children's Defense Fund. (2013). *Every day in America.* www.childrendefense.org. Retrieved April 26, 2013.
2. Thompson, Charles L., Linda B. Rudolph, and Donna Henderson. *Counseling Children,* Sixth Edition. Thomson Brooks/Cole, Belmont, CA. 2004, pg. 9.
3. Military.com. Retrieved from http://www.military.com/Recruiting/Content/0,13898, rec_step01-military
4. Smalley, Gary and John Trent, Ph.D. *The Blessing,* Pocket Books, New York. 1986.
5. Thompson, Charles L., Linda B. Rudolph, and Donna Henderson. *Counseling Children,* Sixth Edition. Thomson Brooks/Cole, Belmont, CA. 2004, pg. 41.
6. *Treatment of Childhood Disorders.*, Mash, Eric J., and Russell A. Barkley. 2006. Copyright Guilford Press. Preprinted with permission of The Guilford Press., pg. 67.
7. Ibid., pgs. 67-68.
8. Ibid., pg. 72.
9. Nickelodeon ParentsConnect. (11 March, 2013). Retrieved from http://babynamesworld.parentsconnect.com/meaning_of_Simon.html
10. Biblical-Baby-Names.com. (11 March, 2013). Retrieved from http://www.biblical-baby-names.com/search.html
11. Biblical-Baby-Names.com. (11 March, 2013). Retrieved from http://www.biblical-baby-names.com/search.html?st=begin&sn=peter
12. Mash, op. cit., pgs.78-79.
13. Nauert, Rick, Ph. D. Sleep Problems Accompany ADHD. http://psychcentral.com/news/2008/04/09/sleep-problems-accompany-adhd/2134.html 14 July, 2008.
14. Dodson, William, M. D. Treating ADHD with a Better Night's Sleep. ADDitudeMag.com, http:www.additudemag.com/adhd/article/757.html. 14 July, 2008.
15. Greene, Alan, M. D. Sleep Deprivation and ADHD. drgreene.com. http://www.drgreene.org/blank.cfm?print=yest&id=21&action=detail&ref=621 14 July, 2008.
16. *The New England Primer.* "Evening Prayer For a Child." 1843.
17. Numeroff, Laura. *If You Give a Mouse a Cookie.* HarperCollins. 8 May, 1985.